32.85

6/28/07

SCIENTIFIC AMERICAN™

Critical Anthologies on Environment and Climate™

CRITICAL PERSPECTIVES ON
NATURAL DISASTERS

Edited by Jennifer L. Viegas

The Rosen Publishing Group, Inc., New York

Published in 2007 by The Rosen Publishing Group, Inc.
29 East 21st Street, New York, NY 10010

The articles in this book first appeared in the pages of *Scientific American*, as
follows: "Earthquake Conversations" by Ross S. Stein, January 2003; "The
Threat of Silent Earthquakes" by Peter Cervelli, March 2004; "Tsunami!" by
Frank I. González, May 1999; "The Scarred Earth" by Madhusree Mukerjee,
March 2005; "Killer Waves on the East Coast?" by Sarah Simpson, October
2000; "Mount Etna's Ferocious Future" by Tom Pfeiffer, April 2003;
"Volcanic Sniffing" by Charles Choi, November 2004; "Burning Questions"
by Douglas Gantenbein, November 2002; "Disease Dustup" by Otto Pohl,
July 2003; "The Killing Lakes" by Marguerite Holloway, July 2000;
"Dissecting a Hurricane" by Tim Beardsley, March 2000; "Lightning Between
Earth and Space" by Stephen B. Mende, Davis D. Sentman, and Eugene M.
Wescott, August 1997; "Lightning Control with Lasers" by Jean-Claude Diels,
Ralph Bernstein, Karl E. Stahlkopf, and Xin Miao Zhao, August 1997;
"Tornadoes" by Robert Davies-Jones, August 1995; "The Day the World
Burned" by David A. Kring and Daniel D. Durda, December 2003; "Repeated
Blows" by Luann Becker, March 2002; and "The Day the Sands Caught Fire"
by Jeffrey C. Wynn and Eugene M. Shoemaker, November 1998.

First Edition

Library of Congress Cataloging-in-Publication Data

Critical perspectives on natural disasters/edited by Jennifer L. Viegas.—1st ed.
   p. cm.—(Scientific American critical anthologies on environment and
climate)
Includes bibliographical references and index.
ISBN 1-4042-0824-0 (library binding)
1. Natural disasters—Juvenile literature. I. Viegas, Jennifer. II. Series.
GB5019.C75 2007
363.34—dc22

                            2005035518

Manufactured in the United States of America

On the cover: A survivor sits among the debris of houses that were destroyed
in the city of Madras in southern India by a tsunami on December 26, 2004.

CONTENTS

Introduction

A disaster is a sudden event that can lead to loss of lives and property. Humans can inflict disasters upon themselves, such as during a war or some other political conflict involving military action. Nuclear accidents, refinery explosions, and chemical spills are examples of other human-made disasters. The articles that you are about to read, however, cover natural disasters and the events and processes associated with such catastrophes.

We like to think that we have complete control over our lives, but nature is a powerful, ever-present force that we almost take for granted. Consider that at this very minute, you are sitting on the surface of the earth's crust. If a fault line, or a weakness in the crust, exists underneath you or near your area, an earthquake could occur at any time. Even without earthquakes, the entire planet is in constant motion as it orbits the sun and rotates around its own axis.

All sorts of massive rocks and space debris orbit through the galaxy, too. Since the earth first formed 4.5 billion years ago, some of these materials have crashed into it, leaving behind massive craters and possibly wiping out entire species. Many paleontologists (scientists who study fossils to determine facts about prehistoric life-forms), for example, believe that a giant asteroid resulted in the extinction of dinosaurs and other prehistoric creatures. Dinosaurs once were the dominant species on our planet. They dominated the earth for about 160 million years. Anthropologists are not yet certain when humans came on the scene. Most believe we emerged hundreds of thousands of years ago, but not millions of years in the past. Even so, it is overwhelming to fathom that an asteroid could destroy the entire human race in one fell swoop. Most researchers think that such a wipeout is possible but that it will not happen during our lifetimes or anytime soon. In fact, some scientists are working on asteroid busters that promise to break flying space objects into harmless pieces.

Asteroid crashes present a possible, yet remote, threat. It may take hundreds of years for a comet's orbit to cross with that of our planet, but certain volcanoes can erupt repeatedly over just a few years. Mount Etna in Sicily, for example, has become more active in recent decades, prompting geologists to pay more attention to this volcano.

It is doubtful that humans will ever gain complete control over natural processes.

However, we can improve upon our scientific knowledge, which will lead to better disaster responses and preparedness in future. Right now, we are still studying many dynamic natural systems, such as weather patterns. Scientists can provide some idea of what the weather will be like several days in advance. However, such predictions often turn out to be incorrect. Similarly, predictions about earthquakes, volcano eruptions, tornadoes, and even meteor collisions have failed in the past.

Researchers know the basics, but many mysteries remain unsolved. For example, weather experts have noticed that storm clouds change their shape just before a tornado forms. Could these visual changes provide a clue that future devices might monitor to predict tornadoes? We do not know yet, but some scientists risk their lives to find an answer.

Flying into a hurricane is dangerous work, but scientists do just that to monitor wind speed and strength, as well as to study how the atmosphere and ocean dynamics might fuel and create storms. Researchers chase down tornadoes in specially equipped vehicles to learn more about how tornadoes form and travel. Experts even try to simulate natural disasters by creating their own lightning and forest fires in controlled settings. Researchers conduct such studies so that we might learn more about the events that lead to natural disasters. This knowledge then could lead to better predictions, preventative measures, and improved responses.

Already academics have proposed some interesting theories. One of the articles in this anthology discusses how laser beams might act like giant lightning rods that can detect lightning before it hits a dangerous, vulnerable spot, such as a nuclear power plant. The laser might then deflect or diminish the strike. Tests show this could be possible. A study on hurricanes in this volume also led to the recent finding that water droplets suspend in air during a storm and can increase the chances of hurricane formation. Scientists now are examining the use of harmless, environmentally safe surfactants, or substances that can float on water because they are only partially water-compatible. They could be applied to the ocean surface before periods of known storm activity.

Natural disasters affect all of us, either directly or indirectly. It takes only a single event to affect entire families and communities. This point became painfully clear on December 26, 2004, when more than 175,000 people were killed because of a massive tsunami that struck the coastal regions of Southeast Asia, South Asia, and East Africa. The tragedy also left as many as a million people homeless. Two articles in this collection indicate that additional tsunamis have led to even more deaths and caused further damage in various countries. Even the United States is not immune to tsunamis. They have occurred off the coast of Hawaii, and some experts think tsunamis could form along the New Jersey and North Carolina coastlines.

Tsunamis reveal that one natural event can lead to another. In the case of the 2004 tsunami, a tremendous undersea earthquake rocked the Indian Ocean near the Indonesian island of Sumatra. That one jolting episode sent shock waves across thousands of miles of ocean. The energy created water waves that traveled 500 miles per hour. The waves were large enough to swallow entire towns and beaches. The whole planet actually vibrated and then rotated faster because of this one earthquake.

Yet another scare in recent years combines a natural threat with a human one—terrorism. The article "Disease Dustup" discusses how deadly germs can travel in dust from one country to another. Germs in dust from Africa actually blew to England, where they created an epidemic of foot-and-mouth disease. Since dust so success-fully holds germs, bacteria, and fungi, homeland security experts believe that terrorists could unleash germs over a widespread area simply by storing the germs in dust. It may not be possible to stop every terrorist, but data on natural dust events could enable us to better react if terrorists ever launched such an attack.

Often, many of us spend our free time reading books or watching movies and television shows about fictional natural events. Real life, however, is always more surprising and breathtaking than fiction, as you are about to learn. Whether it is a lake than can spew out toxic gas or an earthquake that has the potential of toppling an entire volcanic island, nature never ceases to amaze. Let us hope that we can watch and learn in wonder, instead of falling victim ourselves to a disaster resulting from the impressive forces of nature. —*JV*

1 | Earthquakes and Tsunamis

Earthquakes originate deep in the ground when sections of the earth's crust, which is its rocky outer shell, suddenly break or shift. Usually, earthquakes occur along known weak areas in the crust called fault lines. While shaking of the ground generally does not kill people directly, earthquakes can lead to numerous deaths resulting from collapsed buildings, fires, and other consequences stemming from the natural event.

Scientists cannot yet predict the precise date and time of an earthquake. However, as you will soon read, there is a growing body of evidence that suggests earthquakes are not random events. In the article "Earthquake Conversations," geophysicist Ross Stein presents his theory that stress created or released by a known earthquake can help to predict subsequent events that are not merely aftershocks. For example, he discusses how a 1999 earthquake in Turkey lowered the odds that a similar tremor would strike the area because the shock of the jolt transferred stress to different parts of the earth's crust in Turkey. Similarly, the big 1906 quake in San Francisco *relieved and transferred stress along the San Andreas fault. However, a scary 1989 trembler in northern California indicates that stress might be building again in the area.*

If Stein's theory is correct, it could lead to significant improvements in the way scientists and governments asses an area's earthquake risks. —JV

"Earthquake Conversations"
by Ross S. Stein
Scientific American, **January 2003**

For decades, earthquake experts dreamed of being able to divine the time and place of the world's next disastrous shock. But by the early 1990s the behavior of quake-prone faults had proved so complex that they were forced to conclude that the planet's largest tremors are isolated, random and utterly unpredictable. Most seismologists now assume that once a major earthquake and its expected aftershocks do their damage, the fault will remain quiet until stresses in the earth's crust have time to rebuild, typically over hundreds or thousands of years. A recent discovery—that earthquakes interact in ways never before imagined—is beginning to overturn that assumption.

This insight corroborates the idea that a major shock relieves stress—and thus the likelihood of a second major tremor—in some areas. But it also suggests that the probability of a succeeding earthquake elsewhere along the fault or on a nearby fault can actually jump by as much as a factor of three. To the people who must stand ready to provide emergency services or to those who set prices for insurance premiums, these refined predictions can be critical in determining which of their constituents are most vulnerable.

At the heart of this hypothesis—known as stress triggering—is the realization that faults are unexpectedly responsive to subtle stresses they acquire as neighboring faults shift and shake. Drawing on records of past tremors and novel calculations of fault behavior, my colleagues and I have learned that the stress relieved during an earthquake does not simply dissipate; instead it moves down the fault and concentrates in sites nearby. This jump in stress promotes subsequent tremors. Indeed, studies of about two dozen faults since 1992 have convinced many of us that earthquakes can be triggered even when the stress swells by as little as one eighth the pressure required to inflate a car tire.

Such subtle cause-and-effect relations among large shocks were not thought to exist—and never played into seismic forecasting—until now. As a result, many scientists have been understandably skeptical about embracing this basis for a new approach to forecasting. Nevertheless, the stress-triggering hypothesis has continued to gain credibility through its ability to explain the location and frequency of earthquakes that followed several destructive shocks in California, Japan and Turkey. The hope of furnishing better warnings for such disasters is the primary motivation behind our ongoing quest to interpret these unexpected conversations between earthquakes.

Aftershocks Ignored

Contradicting the nearly universal theory that major earthquakes strike at random was challenging from the start—especially considering that hundreds of scientists searched in vain for more than three decades to find predictable patterns in global earthquake activity, or seismicity. Some investigators looked for changing rates of small tremors or used sensitive instruments to measure the earth's crust as it tilts, stretches and migrates across distances invisible to the naked eye. Others tracked underground movements of gases, fluids and electromagnetic energy or monitored tiny cracks in the rocks to see whether they open or close before large shocks. No matter what the researchers examined, they found little consistency from one major earthquake to another.

Despite such disparities, historical records confirm that about one third of the world's recorded tremors—so-called aftershocks—cluster in space and time. All true aftershocks were thought to hit somewhere along the segment of the fault that slipped during the main shock. Their timing also follows a routine pattern, according to observations first made in 1894 by Japanese seismologist Fusakichi Omori and since developed into a basic principle known as Omori's law. Aftershocks are most abundant immediately after a main shock. Ten days later the rate of aftershocks drops to 10 percent of the initial rate, 100 days later it falls to 1 percent, and so on. This predictable jump and decay in seismicity means that an initial tremor modifies the earth's crust in ways that raise the prospect of succeeding ones, contradicting the view that earthquakes occur randomly in time. But because aftershocks are typically smaller than the most damaging quakes scientists would like to be able to predict, they were long overlooked as a key to unlocking the secrets of seismicity.

Once aftershocks are cast aside, the remaining tremors indeed appear—at least at first glance—to be random. But why ignore the most predictable earthquakes to prove that the rest are without order? My colleagues and I decided to hunt instead for what makes aftershocks so regular. We began our search in one of the world's most seismically active regions—the San Andreas Fault system that runs through California. From local records of earthquakes and aftershocks, we knew that on the day following a magnitude 7.3 event, the chance of another large shock striking within 100 kilometers is nearly 67 percent—20,000 times the likelihood on any other day. Something about the first shock seemed to dramatically increase the odds of subsequent ones, but what?

That big leap in probability explains why no one was initially surprised in June 1992 when a magnitude 6.5 earthquake struck near the southern California town of Big Bear only three hours after a magnitude 7.3 shock occurred 40 kilometers away, near Landers.

(Fortunately, both events took place in the sparsely populated desert and left Los Angeles unscathed.) The puzzling contradiction to prevailing wisdom was that the Big Bear shock struck far from the fault that had slipped during Landers's shaking. Big Bear fit the profile of an aftershock in its timing but not in its location. We suspected that its mysterious placement might hold the clue we were looking for.

By mapping the locations of Landers, Big Bear and hundreds of other California earthquakes, my colleagues and I began to notice a remarkable pattern in the distribution not only of true aftershocks but also of other, smaller earthquakes that follow a main shock by days, weeks or even years. Like the enigmatic Big Bear event, a vast majority of these subsequent tremors tended to cluster in areas far from the fault that slipped during the earthquake and thus far from where aftershocks are supposed to occur. If we could determine what controlled this pattern, we reasoned, the same characteristics might also apply to the main shocks themselves. And if that turned out to be true, we might be well on our way to developing a new strategy for forecasting earthquakes.

Triggers and Shadows

We began by looking at changes within the earth's crust after major earthquakes, which release some of the stress that accumulates slowly as the planet's shifting tectonic plates grind past each other. Along the San Andreas Fault, for instance, the plate carrying

North America is moving south relative to the one that underlies the Pacific Ocean. As the two sides move in opposite directions, shear stress is exerted parallel to the plane of the fault; as the rocks on opposite sides of the fault press against each other, they exert a second stress, perpendicular to the fault plane. When the shear stress exceeds the frictional resistance on the fault or when the stress pressing the two sides of the fault together is eased, the rocks on either side will slip past each other suddenly, releasing tremendous energy in the form of an earthquake. Both components of stress, which when added together are called Coulomb stress, diminish along the segment of the fault that slips. But because that stress cannot simply disappear, we knew it must be redistributed to other points along the same fault or to other faults nearby. We also suspected that this increase in Coulomb stress could be sufficient to trigger earthquakes at those new locations.

Geophysicists had been calculating Coulomb stresses for years, but scientists had never used them to explain seismicity. Their reasoning was simple: they assumed that the changes were too meager to make a difference. Indeed, the amount of stress transferred is generally quite small—less than 3.0 bars, or at most 10 percent of the total change in stress that faults typically experience during an earthquake. I had my doubts about whether this could ever be enough to trigger a fault to fail. But when Geoffrey King of the Paris Geophysical Institute, Jian Lin of the Woods Hole

Oceanographic Institution in Massachusetts and I calculated the areas in southern California where stress had increased after major earthquakes, we were amazed to see that the increases—small though they were—matched clearly with sites where the succeeding tremors had clustered. The implications of this correlation were unmistakable: regions where the stress rises will harbor the majority of subsequent earthquakes, both large and small. We also began to see something equally astonishing: small reductions in stress could inhibit future tremors. On our maps, earthquake activity plummeted in these so-called stress shadows.

Coulomb stress analysis nicely explained the locations of certain earthquakes in the past, but a more important test would be to see whether we could use this new technique to forecast the sites of *future* earthquakes reliably. Six years ago I joined geophysicist James H. Dieterich of the U.S. Geological Survey (USGS) and geologist Aykut A. Barka of Istanbul Technical University to assess Turkey's North Anatolian fault, among the world's most heavily populated fault zones. Based on our calculations of where Coulomb stress had risen as a result of past earthquakes, we estimated that there was a 12 percent chance that a magnitude 7 shock or larger would strike the segment of the fault near the city of Izmit sometime between 1997 and 2027. That may seem like fairly low odds, but in comparison, all but one other segment of the 1,000-kilometer-long fault had odds of only 1 to 2 percent.

Forecasting Under Stress

How people perceive the threat of an earthquake in their part of the world depends in great part on what kind of warnings are presented to them. Most of today's seismic forecasts assume that one earthquake is unrelated to the next. Every fault segment is viewed as having an average time period between tremors of a given size— the larger the shock, the greater the period, for example—but the specific timing of the shocks is believed to be random. The best feature of this method, known as a Poisson probability, is that a forecast can be made without knowing when the last significant earthquake occurred. Seismologists can simply infer the typical time period between major shocks based on geologic records of much older tremors along that segment of the fault. This conservative strategy yields odds that do not change with time.

In contrast, a more refined type of forecast called the renewal probability predicts that the chances of a damaging shock climb as more time passes since the last one struck. These growing odds are based on the assumption that stress along a fault increases gradually in the wake of a major earthquake. My colleagues and I build the probabilities associated with earthquake interactions on top of this second traditional technique by including the effects of stress changes imparted by nearby earthquakes. Comparing the three types of forecasts for Turkey's North Anatolian fault near Istanbul

continued on following page

continued from previous page

illustrates their differences, which are most notable immediately after a major shock.

In the years leading up to the catastrophic Izmit earthquake of August 1999, the renewal probability of a shock of magnitude 7 or greater on the four faults within 50 kilometers of Istanbul had been rising slowly since the last large earthquake struck each of them, between 100 and 500 years ago. According to this type of forecast, the August shock created a sharp drop in the likelihood of a second major tremor in the immediate vicinity of Izmit, because the faults there were thought to have relaxed. But the quake caused no change in the 48 percent chance of severe shaking 100 kilometers to the west, in Istanbul, sometime in the next 30 years. Those odds will continue to grow slowly with time— unlike the Poisson probability, which will remain at only 20 percent regardless of other tremors that may occur near the capital city.

When the effects of my team's new stress-triggering hypothesis were added to the renewal probability, every-thing changed. The most dramatic result was that the likelihood of a second quake rocking Istanbul shot up suddenly because some of the stress relieved near Izmit during the 1999 shock moved westward along the fault and concentrated closer to the city. That means the Izmit shock raised the probability of an Istanbul quake in the next 30 years from 48 percent to 62 percent. This

so-called interaction probability will continue to decrease over time as the renewal probability climbs. The two forecasts will then converge at about 54 percent in the year 2060—assuming the next major earthquake doesn't occur before then.

Predicted odds of a major earthquake striking within 50 kilometers of Istanbul can vary dramatically. The odds, which stay the same or rise slowly with time in traditional forecasts, jump significantly when stresses transferred during the 1999 Izmit earthquake are included.

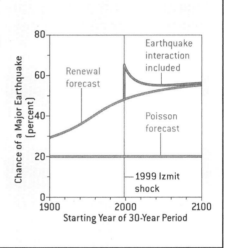

We did not have to wait long for confirmation. In August 1999 a magnitude 7.4 quake devastated Izmit, killing 25,000 people and destroying more than $6.5 billion worth of property. But this earthquake was merely the most recent in a falling-domino-style sequence of 12 major shocks that had struck the North Anatolian fault since 1939. In a particularly brutal five-year period, fully 700 kilometers of the fault slipped in a deadly westward progression of four shocks. We suspected that stress transferred beyond the end of each rupture triggered the successive earthquake, including Izmit's.

In November 1999 the 13th domino fell. Some of the Coulomb stress that had shifted away from the fault segment near Izmit triggered a magnitude 7.1 earthquake near the town of Düzce, about 100 kilometers to the east. Fortunately, Barka had calculated the stress increase resulting from the Izmit shock and had published it in the journal *Science* two months earlier. Barka's announcement had emboldened engineers to close school buildings in Düzce that were lightly damaged by the first shock despite pleas by school officials who said that students had nowhere else to gather for classes. Some of these buildings were flattened by the November shock.

If subsequent calculations by Parsons of the USGS, Shinji Toda of Japan's Active Fault Research Center, Barka, Dieterich and me are correct, that may not be the last of the Izmit quake's aftermath. The stress transferred during that shock has also raised the probability of strong shaking in the nearby capital, Istanbul, sometime this year from 1.9 percent to 4.2 percent. Over the next 30 years we estimate those odds to be 62 percent; if we assumed large shocks occur randomly, the odds would be just 20 percent.

The stress-triggering hypothesis offers some comfort alongside such gloom and doom. When certain regions are put on high alert for earthquakes, the danger inevitably drops in others. In Turkey the regions of reduced concern happen to be sparsely populated relative to Istanbul. But occasionally the opposite is true. One of the most dramatic examples is the relative lack of seismicity that the San Francisco Bay Area, now home to five million people, has experienced since the great magnitude 7.9 earthquake of 1906. A 1998 analysis by my USGS colleagues Ruth A. Harris and Robert W. Simpson demonstrated that the stress shadows of the 1906 shock fell across several parallel strands of the San Andreas Fault in the Bay Area, while the stress increases occurred well to the north and south. This could explain why the rate of damaging shocks in the Bay Area dropped by an order of magnitude compared with the 75 years preceding 1906. Seismicity in the Bay Area is calculated to slowly emerge from this shadow as stress rebuilds on the faults; the collapsed highways and other damage wrought by the 1989 Loma Prieta shock may be a harbinger of this reawakening.

Bolstering the Hypothesis

Examinations of the earthquakes in Turkey and in southern California fortified our assertion that even tiny stress changes can have momentous effects, both calming and catastrophic. But despite the growing number of examples we had to support this idea, one key point was difficult to explain: roughly one quarter of the earthquakes we examined occurred in areas where stress had *decreased*. It was easy for our more skeptical colleagues to argue that no seismicity should occur in these shadow zones, because the main shock would have relieved at least some stress and thus pushed those

Earthquake Clusters

Places where stress jumps after major earthquakes tend to be the sites of subsequent tremors, both large and small. Conversely, few tremors occur where the stress plummets, regardless of the location of nearby faults.

SOUTHERN CALIFORNIA, U.S.

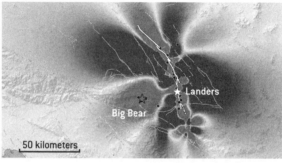

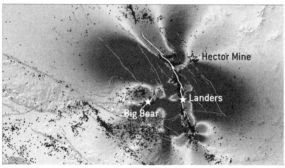

Magnitude 7.3 shock in the southern California desert near Landers in 1992 increased the expected rate of earthquakes to the southwest, where the magnitude 6.5 Big Bear shock struck three hours later (*top*). Stresses imparted by the combination of the Landers and Big Bear events coincided with the regions where the vast

majority of tremors occurred over the next seven years, culminating with the magnitude 7.1 Hector Mine quake in 1999 (*bottom on page 24*).

KAGOSHIMA, JAPAN

Twin earthquakes can turn the rate of earthquake occurrence, or seismicity, up and down in the same spot. In March 1997 a magnitude 6.5 tremor increased stress and seismicity to the west of the ruptured fault (*above left*). Seismicity in that area then dropped along with stress (*above right*) following a magnitude 6.3 shock that struck 48 days later three kilometers to the south.

segments of the fault further from failure. We now have an answer. Seismicity never shuts off completely in the shadow zones, nor does it turn on completely in the trigger zones. Instead the *rate* of seismicity—the number of earthquakes per unit of time—merely drops in the shadows or climbs in the trigger zones relative to the preceding rate in that area.

We owe this persuasive extension of stress triggering to a theory proposed by Dieterich in 1994. Known as rate/state friction, it jettisons the comfortable concept of friction as a property that can only vary between two values—high friction when the material is stationary and lower friction when it is sliding. Rather, faults can become stickier or more slippery as the rate of movement along the fault changes and as the history of motion, or the state, evolves. These conclusions grew out of lab experiments in which Dieterich's team sawed a miniature fault into a Volkswagen-size slab of granite and triggered tiny earthquakes.

When earthquake behavior is calculated with friction as a variable rather than a fixed value, it becomes clear that Omori's law is a fundamental property not just of so-called aftershocks but of *all* earthquakes. The law's prediction that the rate of shocks will first jump and then diminish with time explains why a region does not forever retain the higher rate of seismicity that results from an increase in stress. But that is only half the story. Dieterich's theory reveals a characteristic of the seismicity that Omori's law misses entirely. In areas where a main shock relieves stress, the rate of seismicity immediately plunges but will slowly return to preshock values in a predictable manner. These points may seem subtle, but rate/state friction allowed us for the first time to make predictions of how jumps or declines in seismicity would change over time. When calculating Coulomb stresses alone, we could define the general location of new earthquakes but not their timing.

Our emerging ideas about both the place and the time of stress-triggered earthquakes were further confirmed by a global study conducted early last year. Parsons considered the more than 100 earthquakes of magnitude 7 or greater that have occurred worldwide in the past 25 years and then examined all subsequent shocks of at least magnitude 5 within 250 kilometers of each magnitude 7 event. Among the more than 2,000 shocks in this inventory, 61 percent occurred at sites where a preceding shock increased the stress, even by a small amount. Few of these triggered shocks were close enough to the main earthquake to be considered an aftershock, and in all instances the rate of these triggered tremors decreased in the time period predicted by rate/state friction and Omori's law.

Now that we are regularly incorporating the concept of rate/state friction into our earthquake analyses, we have begun to uncover more sophisticated examples of earthquake interaction than Coulomb stress analyses alone could have illuminated. Until recently, we had explained only relatively simple situations, such as those in California and Turkey, in which a large earthquake spurs seismicity in some areas and makes it sluggish in others. We knew that a more compelling case for the stress-triggering hypothesis would be an example in which successive, similar-size shocks are seen to turn the frequency of earthquakes up and down in the same spot, like a dimmer switch on an electric light.

Toda and I discovered a spectacular example of this phenomenon, which we call toggling seismicity.

Early last year we began analyzing an unusual pair of magnitude 6.5 earthquakes that struck Kagoshima, Japan, in 1997. Immediately following the first earthquake, which occurred in March, a sudden burst of seismicity cropped up in a 25-square-kilometer region just beyond the west end of the failed segment of the fault. When we calculated where the initial earthquake transferred stress, we found that it fell within the same zone as the heightened seismicity. We also found that the rate immediately began decaying just as rate/state friction predicted. But when the second shock struck three kilometers to the south only seven weeks later, the region of heightened seismicity experienced a sudden, additional drop of more than 85 percent. In this case, the trigger zone of the first earthquake had fallen into the shadow zone of the second one. In other words, the first quake turned seismicity up, and the second one turned it back down.

A New Generation of Forecasts

Eavesdropping on the conversations between earthquakes has revealed, if nothing else, that seismicity is highly interactive. And although phenomena other than stress transfer may influence these interactions, my colleagues and I believe that enough evidence exists to warrant an overhaul of traditional probabilistic earthquake forecasts. By refining the likelihood of dangerous tremors to reflect subtle jumps and declines in stress, these new assessments will help governments, the insurance industry and the public at large to better evaluate their earthquake risk. Traditional strategies already make some degree of prioritizing possible, driving the strengthening of buildings and other precautions in certain cities or regions at the expense of others. But our analyses have shown that taking stress triggering into account will raise different faults to the top of the high-alert list than using traditional methods alone will. By the same token, a fault deemed dangerous by traditional practice may actually be a much lower risk.

An important caveat is that any type of earthquake forecast is difficult to prove right and almost impossible to prove wrong. Regardless of the factors that are considered, chance plays a tremendous role in whether a large earthquake occurs, just as it does in whether a particular weather pattern produces a rainstorm. The meteorologists' advantage over earthquake scientists is that they have acquired millions more of the key measurements that help improve their predictions. Weather patterns are much easier to measure than stresses inside the earth, after all, and storms are much more frequent than earthquakes.

Refining earthquake prediction must follow the same path, albeit more slowly. That is why my team has moved forward by building an inventory of forecasts for large earthquakes near the shock-prone cities of Istanbul, Landers, San Francisco and Kobe. We are also gearing up to make assessments for Los Angeles and Tokyo, where a major earthquake could wreak trillion-dollar devastation. Two strong shocks along Alaska's

Denali fault in the fall of 2002—magnitude 6.7 on October 23 and magnitude 7.9 on November 3—appear to be another stress-triggered sequence. Our calculations suggest that the first shock increased the likelihood of the second by a factor of 100 during the intervening 10 days. We are further testing the theory by forecasting smaller, nonthreatening earthquakes, which are more numerous and thus easier to predict.

In the end, the degree to which any probabilistic forecast will protect people and property is still uncertain. But scientists have plenty of reasons to keep pursuing this dream: several hundred million people live and work along the world's most active fault zones. With that much at stake, stress triggering—or any other phenomenon that has the potential to raise the odds of a damaging earthquake—should not be ignored.

The Author

Ross S. Stein is a geophysicist with the U.S. Geological Survey's Earthquake Hazards Team in Menlo Park, Calif. He joined the survey in 1981 after earning a Ph.D. from Stanford University in 1980 and serving as a post-doctoral fellow at Columbia University. Stein's research, which has been devoted to improving scientists' ability to assess earthquake hazards, has been funded by U.S. agencies such as the Office of Foreign Disaster Assistance and by private companies, including the European insurance company Swiss Re. For the work outlined in this article, Stein received the Eugene M. Shoemaker

Distinguished Achievement Award of the USGS in 2000. He also presented the results in his Frontiers of Geophysics Lecture at the annual meeting of the American Geophysical Union in 2001. Stein has appeared in several TV documentaries, including Great Quakes: Turkey *[Learning Channel, 2001].*

Most of us are familiar with rumbling earthquakes that shake houses and rattle nerves, but a new threat is coming to light—silent earthquakes. People standing over such an earthquake may not detect any shaking because the activity is happening away from the ground surface. In fact, it was only just over a decade ago that researchers began to monitor silent earthquakes closely using Global Positioning System receivers, similar to the kind used by skiers and hikers who need to track their locations in wilderness areas.

Peter Cervelli works as a geologist in Hawaii, where silent quakes are very common due to seafloor movements, volcanic activity, and the presence of numerous faults. He outlines the hazards of this newly understood phenomenon in the following article. As Cervelli explains, water, such as from a heavy rainstorm, can seep into fault zones and, if the pressure is high enough, the water can push the two sides of the fault apart. Although most silent quakes result in little or no damage on the earth's surface, Cervelli presents an ominous scenario. He believes that if a silent earthquake struck underneath a volcano, such as Hawaii's mammoth Kilauea, the weakly structured volcano could collapse and slide, possibly triggering destructive tsunamis or larger regular earthquakes. —JV

"The Threat of Silent Earthquakes"
by Peter Cervelli
Scientific American, March 2004

In early November 2000 the Big Island of Hawaii experienced its largest earthquake in more than a decade. Some 2,000 cubic kilometers of the southern slope of Kilauea volcano lurched toward the ocean, releasing the energy of a magnitude 5.7 shock. Part of that motion took place under an area where thousands of people stop every day to catch a glimpse of one of the island's most spectacular lava flows. Yet when the earthquake struck, no one noticed—not even seismologists.

How could such a notable event be overlooked? As it turns out, quaking is not an intrinsic part of all earthquakes. The event on Kilauea was one of the first unambiguous records of a so-called silent earthquake, a type of massive earth movement unknown to science until just a few years ago. Indeed, I would never have discovered this quake if my colleagues at the

U.S. Geological Survey's Hawaiian Volcano Observatory had not already been using a network of sensitive instruments to monitor the volcano's activity. When I finally noticed that Kilauea's south flank had shifted 10 centimeters along an underground fault, I also saw that this movement had taken nearly 36 hours—a turtle's pace for an earthquake. In a typical tremor, opposite sides of the fault rocket past each other in a matter of seconds—quickly enough to create the seismic waves that cause the ground to rumble and shake.

But just because an earthquake happens slowly and quietly does not make it insignificant. My co-investigators and I realized immediately that Kilauea's silent earthquake could be a harbinger of disaster. If that same large body of rock and debris were to gain momentum and take the form of a gigantic landslide—separating itself from the rest of the volcano and sliding rapidly into the sea—the consequences would be devastating. The collapsing material would push seawater into towering tsunami waves that could threaten coastal cities along the entire Pacific Rim. Such catastrophic flank failure, as geologists call it, is a potential threat around many island volcanoes worldwide.

Unexpected Stir

Fortunately, the discovery of silent earthquakes is revealing more good news than bad. The chances of catastrophic flank failure are slim, and the instruments that record silent earthquakes might make early warnings possible. New evidence for conditions that might trigger silent slip suggests bold strategies for preventing flank collapse. Occurrences of silent earthquakes are also being reported in areas where flank failure is not an issue. There silent earthquakes are inspiring ways to improve forecasts of their ground-shaking counterparts.

The discovery of silent earthquakes and their link to catastrophic flank collapse was a by-product of efforts to study other potential natural hazards. Destructive earthquakes and volcanoes are a concern in Japan and the U.S. Pacific Northwest, where tectonic plates constantly plunge deep into the earth along what are called subduction zones. Beginning in the early 1990s, geologists began deploying large networks of continuously recording Global Positioning System (GPS) receivers in these regions and along the slopes of active volcanoes, such as Kilauea. By receiving signals from a constellation of more than 30 navigational satellites, these instruments can measure their own positions on the planet's surface at any given time to within a few millimeters.

The scientists who deployed these GPS receivers expected to see both the slow, relentless motion of the planet's shell of tectonic plates and the relatively quick movements that earthquakes and volcanoes trigger. It came as some surprise when these instruments detected small ground movements that were not associated with any known earthquake or eruption. When researchers plotted the ground movements on a map, the pattern that resulted very much resembled one characteristic of fault movement. In other words, all the GPS stations on one side of a given fault moved several centimeters in the same general direction. This pattern would have been no surprise if it had taken a year or longer to form. In that case, scientists would have known that a slow and steady process called fault creep was responsible. But at rates of up to centimeters a day, the mystery events were hundreds of times as fast as that. Beyond their relative speediness, these silent earthquakes shared another attribute with their noisy counterparts that distinguished them from fault creep: they are not steady processes but instead are discrete events that begin and end suddenly.

That sudden beginning, when it takes place on the slopes of a volcanic island, creates concern about a possible catastrophic flank event. Most typical earthquakes happen along faults that have built-in brakes: motion stops once the stress is relieved between the two chunks of earth that are trying to move past each other. But activity may not stop if gravity becomes the primary driver. In the worst-case scenario, the section of the volcano lying above the fault becomes so unstable that once slip starts, gravity pulls the entire mountainside downhill until it disintegrates into a pile of debris on the ocean floor.

The slopes of volcanoes such as Kilauea become steep and vulnerable to this kind of collapse when the lava from repeated eruptions builds them up more rapidly than they can erode away. Discovering the silent earthquake on Kilauea suggests that the volcano's south flank is on the move—perhaps on its way to eventual obliteration.

For now, friction along the fault is acting like an emergency brake. But gravity has won out in many other instances in the past. Scientists have long seen evidence of ancient collapses in sonar images of giant debris fields in the shallow waters surrounding volcanic islands around the world, including Majorca in the Mediterranean Sea and the Canary Islands in the Atlantic Ocean. In the Hawaiian Islands, geologists have found more than 25 individual collapses that have occurred over the past five million years—the blink of an eye in geologic time.

In a typical slide, the volume of material that enters the ocean is hundreds of times as great as the section of Mount St. Helens that blew apart during the 1980 eruption—more than enough to have triggered immense tsunamis. On the Hawaiian island of Lanai, for instance, geologists discovered evidence of wave action, including abundant marine shell fragments, at elevations of 325 meters. Gary M. McMurtry of the University of Hawaii at Manoa and his colleagues conclude that the most likely way the shells could have reached such a lofty location was within the waves of a tsunami that attained the astonishing height of 300 meters along some Hawaiian coastlines. Most of the tallest waves recorded in modern times were no more than one tenth that size.

Preparing for the Worst

As frightening as such an event may sound, this hazard must be understood in the proper context. Catastrophic failure of volcanic slopes is very rare on a human timescale—though far more common than the potential for a large asteroid or comet to have a damaging collision with the earth. Collapses large enough to generate a tsunami occur somewhere in the Hawaiian Islands only about once every 100,000 years. Some scientists estimate that such events occur worldwide once every 10,000 years. Because the hazard is extremely destructive when it does happen, many scientists agree that it is worth preparing for.

To detect deformation within unstable volcanic islands, networks of continuous GPS receivers are beginning to be deployed on Réunion Island in the Indian Ocean, on Fogo in the Cape Verde Islands, and throughout the Galápagos archipelago, among others. Kilauea's network of more than 20 GPS stations, for example, has already revealed that the volcano experiences creep, silent earthquakes as well as large, destructive typical earthquakes. Some scientists propose, however, that Kilauea may currently be protected from catastrophic collapse by several underwater piles of mud and rock—probably debris from old flank collapses—that are buttressing its south flank. New discoveries about the way Kilauea is slipping can be easily generalized to other island volcanoes that may not have similar buttressing structures.

The Mechanics of Silent Earthquakes

Percolating water may trigger silent earthquakes if it finds a way into a vulnerable fault. Highly pressurized by the burden of overlying rock, water can push apart the two sides of the fault (*inset*), making it easier for them to slip past each other (*arrows*). This kind of silent slip can occur within subduction zones and volcanic islands.

SUBDUCTION ZONE   **VOLCANIC ISLAND**

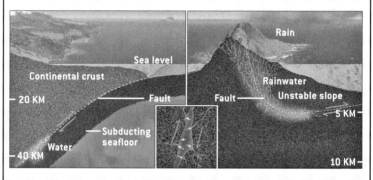

Water squeezed out of hydrous minerals in a slab of ancient seafloor may enter faults created as the slab dives underneath another tectonic plate.	**Water-filled fault**	Rainwater may seep down from the earth's surface into shallow faults, such as those that separate an unstable slope from the rest of a volcano.

Whatever the specific circumstances for an island, the transition from silent slip to abrupt collapse would involve a sudden acceleration of the mobile slope. In the worst case, this acceleration would proceed immediately to breakneck velocities, leaving no chance for early detection and warning. In the best case, the acceleration would occur in fits and starts, in a cascade of silent earthquakes slowly escalating into regular earthquakes, and then on to catastrophe. A continuous GPS network could easily detect this fitful acceleration, well before ground-shaking earthquakes began to occur and, with luck, in plenty of time for a useful tsunami warning.

If the collapse were big enough, however, a few hours' or even days' warning might come as little comfort because it would be so difficult at that point to evacuate everyone. This problem raises the question of whether authorities might ever implement preventive measures. The problem of stabilizing the teetering flanks of oceanic volcanoes is solvable—in principle. In practice, however, the effort required would be immense. Consider simple brute force. If enough rock were removed from the upper reaches of an unstable volcanic flank, then the gravitational potential energy that is driving the system toward collapse would disappear for at least several hundred thousand years. A second possible method—lowering an unstable flank slowly through a series of small earthquakes—would be much cheaper but fraught with geologic unknowns and potential dangers. To do so, scientists could conceivably harness as a tool to prevent collapse the very thing that may be currently driving silent earthquakes on Kilauea.

Nine days before the most recent silent earthquake on Kilauea, a torrential rainstorm dropped nearly a meter of water on the volcano in less than 36 hours. Geologists have long known that water leaking into faults can trigger earthquakes, and nine days is about the same amount of time that they estimate it takes water to work its way down through cracks and pores in Kilauea's fractured basaltic rock to a depth of five kilometers—where the silent earthquake occurred. My colleagues and I suspect that the burden of the overlying rock pressurized the rainwater, forcing the sides of the fault apart and making it much easier for them to slip past each other.

This discovery lends credence to the controversial idea of forcefully injecting water or steam into faults at the base of an unstable flank to trigger the stress-relieving earthquakes needed to let it down slowly. This kind of human-induced slip happens at very small scales all the time at geothermal plants and other locations where water is pumped into the earth. But when it comes to volcanoes, the extreme difficulty lies in putting the right amount of fluid in the right place so as not to inadvertently generate the very collapse that is meant to be avoided. Some geophysicists considered this strategy as a way to relieve stress along California's infamous San Andreas fault, but they ultimately abandoned the idea for fear that it would create more problems than it would solve.

Wedges of Water

Apart from calling attention to the phenomenon of catastrophic collapse of the flank of a volcano, the discovery of silent earthquakes is forcing scientists to reconsider various aspects of fault motion—including seismic hazard assessments. In the U.S. Pacific Northwest, investigators have observed many silent earthquakes along the enormous Cascadia fault zone between the North American plate and the subducting Juan de Fuca plate. One curious feature of these silent earthquakes is that they happen at regular intervals— so regular, in fact, that scientists are now predicting their occurrence successfully.

This predictability most likely stems from the fact that water flowing from below subduction zones may exert significant control over when and where these faults slip silently. As the subducting plate sinks deeper into the earth, it encounters higher and higher temperatures and pressures, which release the significant amount of water trapped in waterrich minerals that exist within the slab. The silent earthquakes may then take place when a batch of fluid from the slab is working its way up—as the fluid passes, it will unclamp the fault zone a little bit, perhaps allowing some slow slip.

What is more, Garry Rogers and Herb Dragert of the Geological Survey of Canada reported last June that these silent tremors might even serve as precursors to some of the region's large, ground-shaking shocks. Because the slow slips occur deep and at discrete intervals, they regulate the rate at which stress accumulates on the shallower part of the fault zone, which moves in fits and starts. In this shallow, locked segment of the fault, it usually takes years or even centuries to amass the stress required to set off a major shock. Rogers and Dragert suggest, however, that silent slip may dramatically hasten this stress buildup, thereby increasing the risk of a regular earthquake in the weeks and months after a silent one.

Silent earthquakes are forcing scientists to rethink seismic forecasts in other parts of the world as well. Regions of Japan near several so-called seismic gaps—areas where fewer than expected regular earthquakes occur in an otherwise seismically active region—are thought to be overdue for a destructive shock. But if silent slip has been relieving stress along these faults without scientists realizing it, then the degree of danger may actually be less than they think. Likewise, if silent slip is discovered along faults that were considered inactive up to now, these structures will need careful evaluation to determine whether they are also capable of destructive earthquakes.

If future study reveals silent earthquakes to be a common feature of most large faults, then scientists will be forced to revisit long-held doctrines about all earthquakes. The observation of many different speeds of fault slip poses a real challenge to theorists trying to explain the faulting process with fundamental physical laws, for example. It is now believed that the number and sizes of observed earthquakes can be explained with a fairly simple friction law. But can this law also account for silent earthquakes? So far no definitive answer has been found, but research continues.

Silent earthquakes are only just beginning to enter the public lexicon. These subtle events portend an exponential increase in our understanding of the how and why of fault slip. The importance of deciphering fault slip is difficult to overstate because when faults slip quickly, they can cause immense damage, sometimes at a great distance from the source. The existence of silent earthquakes gives scientists a completely new angle on the slip process by permitting the detailed study of fault zones through every stage of their movement.

The Author

Peter Cervelli is a research geophysicist at the U.S. Geological Survey's Hawaiian Volcano Observatory, which sits along the rim of Kilauea Caldera on the Big Island. As leader of the observatory's crustal deformation project, Cervelli is responsible for interpreting data from a network of nearly 50 instruments that measure the tilt, strain and subtle movements within the island's two most active volcanoes, Mauna Loa and Kilauea. Cervelli discovered the silent earthquake that struck Kilauea's south flank in November 2000 while he was working on his Ph.D., which he received from Stanford University in 2001.

The 2004 tsunami seems like an isolated event, but as you will read in this next piece, a number

*of other tsunamis struck various areas in the
1990s. The following article provides an excellent
overview that utilizes both a layman's and a
scientist's perspective. In terms of pure science,
you will learn that tsunamis are remarkable
forces that can swallow lighthouses and engulf
entire beaches. Author Frank González, who is
one of the world's leading tsunami experts,
explains how in just three stages, a calm body of
water can turn into a rippling mass of energy.*

*González also relates, with graphic clarity,
the horror that tsunamis can leave in their aftermath. For example, many victims of the 1998
Papua New Guinea tsunami were trapped by the
water and simply could not flee. The author relates
what it is like to experience such a natural disaster.
He also shows that there is some hope for the
future. Researchers have had some success in
predicting tsunamis using detectors that can
measure earthquakes under the sea. It is likely
that now, after the 2004 tsunami, more work will
be done to implement such systems and to
educate the public about tsunami risks. —JV*

"Tsunami!"
by Frank I. González
Scientific American, May 1999

The sun had set 12 minutes earlier, and twilight was
waning on the northern coast of Papua New Guinea.

It was July 17, 1998, and another tranquil Friday evening was drawing to a close for the men, women and children of Sissano, Arop, Warapu and other small villages on the peaceful sand spit between Sissano Lagoon and the Bismarck Sea. But deep in the earth, far beneath the wooden huts of the unsuspecting villagers, tremendous forces had strained the underlying rock for years. Now, in the space of minutes, this pent-up energy violently released as a magnitude 7.1 earthquake. At 6:49 PM the main shock rocked 30 kilometers (nearly 19 miles) of coastline centered on the lagoon and suddenly deformed the offshore ocean bottom. The normally flat sea surface lurched upward in response, giving birth to a fearsome tsunami.

Retired Colonel John Sanawe, who lived near the southeast end of the sandbar at Arop, survived the tsunami and later told his story to Hugh Davies of the University of Papua New Guinea. Just after the main shock struck only 20 kilometers offshore, Sanawe saw the sea rise above the horizon and then spray vertically perhaps 30 meters. Unexpected sounds—first like distant thunder, then like a nearby helicopter—gradually faded as he watched the sea slowly recede below the normal low-water mark. After four or five minutes of silence, he heard a rumble like that of a low-flying jet plane. Sanawe spotted the first tsunami wave, perhaps three or four meters high. He tried to run home, but the wave overtook him. A second, larger wave flattened the village and swept him a kilometer into a mangrove forest on the inland shore of the lagoon.

Other villagers were not so fortunate as Sanawe. Some were swept across the lagoon and impaled on the broken mangrove branches. Many more were viciously battered by debris. At least 30 survivors would lose injured limbs to gangrene. Saltwater crocodiles and wild dogs preyed on the dead before help could arrive, making it more difficult to arrive at an exact death toll. It now appears that the tsunami killed more than 2,200 villagers, including more than 230 children. Waves up to 15 meters high, which struck within 15 minutes of the main shock, had caught many coastal inhabitants unawares. Of the few villagers who knew of the tsunami hazard, those trapped on the sandbar simply had no safe place to flee.

Tsunamis such as those that pounded Papua New Guinea are the world's most powerful waves. Historical patterns of their occurrence are revealed in large databases developed by James F. Lander, Patricia A. Lockridge and their colleagues at the National Geophysical Data Center in Boulder, Colo., and Viacheslav K. Gusiakov and his associates at the Tsunami Laboratory in Novosibirsk, Russia. Most tsunamis afflict the Pacific Ocean, and 86 percent of those are the products of undersea earthquakes around the Pacific Rim, where powerful collisions of tectonic plates form highly seismic subduction zones.

Since 1990, 10 tsunamis have taken more than 4,000 lives. In all, 82 were reported worldwide—a rate much higher than the historical average of 57 a decade. The increase in tsunamis reported is due to improved global communications; the high death tolls

Larger Wave Than Expected

PAPUA NEW GUINEA
July 17, 1998
Maximum wave height: 15 meters
Fatalities: More than 2,200

Swept clean by three monstrous waves, [the Sissano area,] now a barren sandbar along Papua New Guinea's north coast, once was crowded with houses and villages. Surprisingly, a relatively small earthquake (magnitude 7.1) spawned waves usually limited to much larger quakes. This apparent discrepancy between earthquake strength and tsunami intensity has prompted speculation among scientists that the seismic vibrations may have triggered other seafloor disturbances, such as an underwater landslide or an explosion of gas hydrates, that helped to create a much larger tsunami.

Unexpectedly high tsunami waves have caused other disasters, such as that in Nicaragua in 1992, but intensive surveys of the seafloor to investigate the mystery have never been conducted until now. Two expeditions explored the seafloor off the ravaged coast of Papua New Guinea for signs of an undersea landslide earlier this year. The survey teams, jointly led by Takeshi Matsumoto of the Japan Marine Science and Technology Center and David Tappin of the South Pacific Applied Geoscience Commission, identified a small depression that could be a candidate landslide site. The next question is whether this feature is fresh or was created by another earthquake long ago.

are partly due to increases in coastal populations. My colleagues and I at the National Oceanic and Atmospheric Administration Pacific Marine Environmental Laboratory in Seattle set up an electronic-mail network as a way for researchers in distant parts of the world to help one another make faster and more accurate tsunami surveys. This Tsunami Bulletin Board, now managed by the International Tsunami Information Center, has facilitated communication among tsunami scientists since shortly after the 1992 Nicaragua tsunami.

Disasters similar to those in Nicaragua and Papua New Guinea have wreaked havoc in Hawaii and Alaska in the past, but most tsunami researchers had long believed that the U.S. West Coast was relatively safe from the most devastating events. New evidence now suggests that earthquakes may give birth to large tsunamis every 300 to 700 years along the Cascadia subduction zone, an area off the Pacific Northwest coast where a crustal plate carrying part of the Pacific Ocean is diving under North America. A clear reminder of this particular threat occurred in April 1992, when a magnitude 7.1 earthquake at the southern end of the subduction zone generated a small tsunami near Cape Mendocino, Calif. This event served as the wake-up call that has driven the development of the first systematic national effort to prepare for dangerous tsunamis before they strike. The Pacific Marine Environmental Laboratory is playing a key research and management role in this endeavor.

The Physics of Tsunamis

To understand tsunamis, it is first helpful to distinguish them from wind-generated waves or tides. Breezes blowing across the ocean crinkle the surface into relatively short waves that create currents restricted to a shallow layer; a scuba diver, for example, might easily swim deep enough to find calm water. Strong gales are able to whip up waves 30 meters or higher in the open ocean, but even these do not move deep water.

Tides, which sweep around the globe twice a day, do produce currents that reach the ocean bottom—just as tsunamis do. Unlike true tidal waves, however, tsunamis are not generated by the gravitational pull of the moon or sun. A tsunami is produced impulsively by an undersea earthquake or, much less frequently, by volcanic eruptions, meteorite impacts or underwater landslides. With speeds that can exceed 700 kilometers per hour in the deep ocean, a tsunami wave could easily keep pace with a Boeing 747. Despite its high speed, a tsunami is not dangerous in deep water. A single wave is less than a few meters high, and its length can extend more than 750 kilometers in the open ocean. This creates a sea-surface slope so gentle that the wave usually passes unnoticed in deep water. In fact, the Japanese word *tsu-nami* translates literally as "harbor wave," perhaps because a tsunami can speed silently and undetected across the ocean, then unexpectedly arise as destructively high waves in shallow coastal waters.

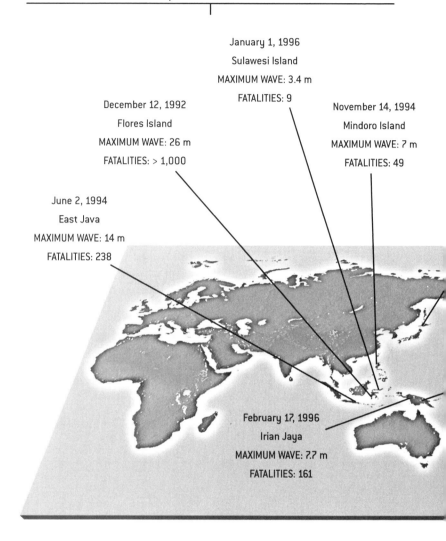

January 1, 1996
Sulawesi Island
MAXIMUM WAVE: 3.4 m
FATALITIES: 9

December 12, 1992
Flores Island
MAXIMUM WAVE: 26 m
FATALITIES: > 1,000

November 14, 1994
Mindoro Island
MAXIMUM WAVE: 7 m
FATALITIES: 49

June 2, 1994
East Java
MAXIMUM WAVE: 14 m
FATALITIES: 238

February 17, 1996
Irian Jaya
MAXIMUM WAVE: 7.7 m
FATALITIES: 161

A powerful tsunami also has a very long reach: it can transport destructive energy from its source to coastlines thousands of kilometers away. Hawaii, because of its midocean location, is especially vulnerable to such Pacific-wide tsunamis. Twelve damaging tsunamis have struck Hawaii since 1895. In the most destructive, 159 people died there in 1946 from killer

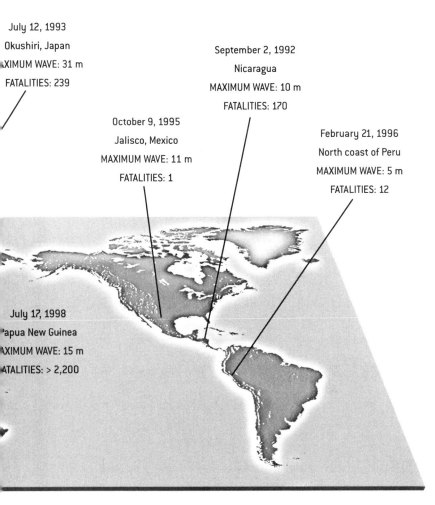

July 12, 1993
Okushiri, Japan
XIMUM WAVE: 31 m
FATALITIES: 239

September 2, 1992
Nicaragua
MAXIMUM WAVE: 10 m
FATALITIES: 170

October 9, 1995
Jalisco, Mexico
MAXIMUM WAVE: 11 m
FATALITIES: 1

February 21, 1996
North coast of Peru
MAXIMUM WAVE: 5 m
FATALITIES: 12

July 17, 1998
Papua New Guinea
XIMUM WAVE: 15 m
ATALITIES: > 2,200

Ten destructive Tsunamis have claimed more than 4,000 lives since
1990. Last year's Papua New Guinea disaster is the most recent in
this string of killer waves generated by earthquakes along colliding
tectonic plates of the Pacific Rim.

waves generated almost 3,700 kilometers away in
Alaska's Aleutian Islands. Such remote-source tsunamis
can strike unexpectedly, but local-source tsunamis—as

Slow, Silent, Deadly Quake

NICARAGUA
September 2, 1992
Maximum wave height: 10 meters
Fatalities: 170

Coastal inhabitants can be educated to run to higher ground when they feel the land shake from an earthquake. But in certain tragic cases, such as the 1992 Nicaragua tsunami that killed 170 people and left 13,000 homeless, residents feel only a minor tremor, or even none at all, and assume there is no danger. An estimated 5 to 10 percent of tsunami-causing earthquakes are of this particularly hazardous breed—so-called silent earthquakes, first described by Hiroo Kanamori of the California Institute of Technology.

In the latest Nicaragua event, the short waves that produce the characteristic rumbling of an earthquake—and that die out quickly as they spread out from the epicenter—never made it from the quake's offshore origin to the mainland. Longer waves did reach the coast, but they hardly shook the ground. What is more, standard seismometers, which record only seismic waves with periods less than 20 seconds, missed most of these longer waves. Kanamori argued that the Nicaragua quake was actually five times greater than its assigned magnitude of 7.0 because these low-frequency waves had been ignored. The Nicaragua event made it abundantly clear that broadband seismometers sensitive to low-frequency waves must be linked to warning systems to forecast the true potential tsunami danger.

in the case of last year's Papua New Guinea disaster—can be especially devastating. Lander has estimated that more than 90 percent of all fatalities occur within about 200 kilometers of the source. As an extreme example, it is believed that a tsunami killed more than 30,000 people within 120 kilometers of the catastrophic eruption of Krakatoa volcano in the Sunda Straits of Indonesia in 1883. That explosion generated waves as high as a 12-story building.

Regardless of their origin, tsunamis evolve through three overlapping but quite distinct physical processes: generation by any force that disturbs the water column, propagation from deeper water near the source to shallow coastal areas and, finally, inundation of dry land. Of these, the propagation phase is best understood, whereas generation and inundation are more difficult to model with computer simulations. Accurate simulations are important in predicting where future remote-source tsunamis will strike and in guiding disaster surveys and rescue efforts, which must concentrate their resources on regions believed to be hardest hit.

Generation is the process by which a seafloor disturbance, such as movement along a fault, reshapes the sea surface into a tsunami. Modelers assume that this sea-surface displacement is identical to that of the ocean bottom, but direct measurements of seafloor motion have never been available (and may never be). Instead researchers use an idealized model of the quake: they assume that the crustal plates slip past one another along a simple, rectangular plane inside the earth. Even then, predicting the tsunami's initial height requires at least 10 descriptive parameters, including the amount of slip on each side of the imaginary plane and its length and width. As modelers scramble to guide tsunami survey teams immediately after an earthquake, only the orientation of the assumed fault plane and the quake's location, magnitude and depth can be interpreted from the seismic data alone. All other parameters must be estimated. As a consequence, this first simulation frequently underestimates inundation, sometimes by factors of 5 or 10.

Low inundation estimates can signify that the initial tsunami height was also understated because the single-plane fault model distributes seismic energy over too large an area. Analyses of seismic data cannot resolve energy distribution patterns any shorter than the seismic waves themselves, which extend for several hundred kilometers. But long after the tsunami strikes land, modelers can work backward from records of run-up and additional earthquake data to refine the tsunami's initial height. For example, months of aftershocks eventually reveal patterns of seismic energy that are concentrated in regions much smaller than the original, single-plane fault model assumed. When seismic energy is focused in a smaller area, the vertical motion of the seafloor—and therefore the initial tsunami height—is greater. Satisfactory simulations are achieved only after months of labor-intensive work, but every simulation that matches the real disaster improves scientists' ability to make better predictions.

Propagation of the tsunami transports seismic energy away from the earthquake site through undulations of the water, just as shaking moves the energy through the earth. At this point, the wave height is so small compared with both the wavelength and the water depth that researchers apply linear wave theory, which assumes that the height itself does not affect the wave's behavior. The theory predicts that the deeper the water and the longer the wave, the faster the tsunami. This dependence of wave speed on water depth means that refraction by bumps and grooves on the seafloor can shift the wave's direction, especially as it travels into shallow water. In particular, wave fronts tend to align parallel to the shoreline so that they wrap around a protruding headland before smashing into it with greatly focused incident energy. At the same time, each individual wave must also slow down because of the decreasing water depth, so they begin to overtake one another, decreasing the distance between them in

Tsunamis Evolve

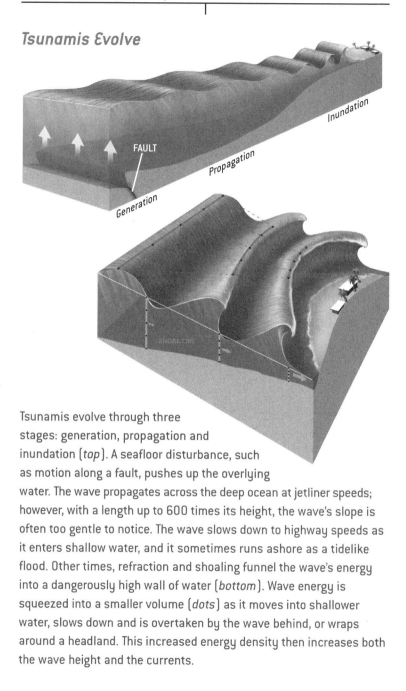

Tsunamis evolve through three stages: generation, propagation and inundation (*top*). A seafloor disturbance, such as motion along a fault, pushes up the overlying water. The wave propagates across the deep ocean at jetliner speeds; however, with a length up to 600 times its height, the wave's slope is often too gentle to notice. The wave slows down to highway speeds as it enters shallow water, and it sometimes runs ashore as a tidelike flood. Other times, refraction and shoaling funnel the wave's energy into a dangerously high wall of water (*bottom*). Wave energy is squeezed into a smaller volume (*dots*) as it moves into shallower water, slows down and is overtaken by the wave behind, or wraps around a headland. This increased energy density then increases both the wave height and the currents.

a process called shoaling. Refraction and shoaling squeeze the same amount of energy into a smaller volume of water, creating higher waves and faster currents.

The last stage of evolution, inundation and run-up, in which a tsunami may run ashore as a breaking wave, a wall of water or a tidelike flood, is perhaps the most difficult to model. The wave height is now so large that linear theory fails to describe the complicated interaction between the water and the shoreline. Vertical run-up can reach tens of meters, but it typically takes only two to three meters to cause damage. Horizontal inundation, if unimpeded by coastal cliffs or other steep topography, can penetrate hundreds of meters inland. Both kinds of flooding are aided and abetted by the typical crustal displacement of a subduction zone earthquake, which lifts the offshore ocean bottom and lowers the land along the coast. This type of displacement propagates waves seaward with a leading crest and landward with a leading trough (the reason a receding sea sometimes precedes a tsunami). Not only does the near-shore subsidence facilitate tsunami penetration inland but, according to recent studies by Raissa Mazova of the Nizhny Novgorod State Technical University in Russia and by Costas Synolakis of the University of Southern California, both theoretical predictions and field surveys indicate that coastal run-up and inundation will be greater if the trough of the leading wave precedes the crest.

Tsunami Threats

Predicting where a tsunami may strike helps to save lives and property only if coastal inhabitants recognize the threat and respond appropriately. More than a quarter of all reliably reported Pacific tsunamis since 1895 originated near Japan. This is not surprising, because Japan is precariously situated near the colliding margins of four tectonic plates. Recognizing the recurring threat, the Japanese have invested heavily over the years in tsunami hazard mitigation, including comprehensive educational and public outreach programs, an effective warning system, shoreline barrier forests, seawalls and other coastal fortifications.

On the night of July 12, 1993, their preparations faced a brutal test. A magnitude 7.8 earthquake in the Sea of Japan generated a tsunami that struck various parts of the small island of Okushiri. Five minutes after the main shock the Japan Meteorological Agency issued a warning over television and radio that a major tsunami was on its way. By then, 10- to 20-meter waves had struck the coastline nearest the source, claiming a number of victims before they could flee. In Aonae, a small fishing village on the island's southern peninsula, many of the 1,600 townspeople fled to high ground as soon as they felt the main shock. A few minutes later tsunami waves five to 10 meters high ravaged hundreds of their homes and businesses and swept them out to sea. More than 200 lives were lost in this disaster, but quick response saved many more.

Over the past century in Japan, approximately 15 percent of 150 tsunamis were damaging or fatal. That track record is much better than the tally in countries with few or no community education programs in place. For example, more than half of the 34 tsunamis that struck Indonesia in the past 100 years were damaging or fatal. Interviews conducted after the 1992 Flores Island tsunami that killed more than 1,000 people indicated that most coastal residents did not recognize the earthquake as the natural warning of a possible tsunami and did not flee inland. Similarly, Papua New Guinea residents were tragically uninformed, sending the number of casualties from last year's disaster higher than expected for a tsunami of that size. A large quake in 1907 evidently lowered the area that is now Sissano Lagoon, but any resulting tsunami was too small and too long ago to imprint a community memory. When the earthquake struck last year, some people actually walked to the coast to investigate the disturbance, thus sealing their fate.

Scientists have learned a great deal from recent tsunamis, but centuries-old waves continue to yield valuable insights. Lander and his colleagues have described more than 200 tsunamis known to have affected the U.S. since the time of the first written records in Alaska and the Caribbean during the early 1700s and in Hawaii and along the West Coast later that century. Total damage is estimated at half a billion dollars and 470 casualties, primarily in Alaska and Hawaii. An immediate threat to those states and the

Education Saves Lives

OKUSHIRI, JAPAN
July 12, 1993
Maximum wave height: 31 meters
Fatalities: 239

Fires burned across the ravaged shores of Aonae, a small fishing village on Okushiri's southern peninsula, in the wake of the 1993 tsunami. Waves ranging from 5 to 10 meters had crashed ashore less than five minutes after the magnitude 7.8 earthquake struck perhaps 15 to 30 kilometers offshore in the Sea of Japan. The waves washed over seawalls erected after past tsunami disasters. High currents swept up buildings, vehicles, docked vessels and heavy material at coastal storage areas, transforming them into waterborne battering rams that obliterated all in their path. Collisions sparked electrical and propane gas fires, but access by fire engines was blocked by debris.

The loss of lives in this event was a great tragedy, but it is clear that both warning technology and community education greatly reduced the number of casualties. The Japan Meteorological Agency issued timely and accurate warnings, and many residents saved themselves by fleeing to high ground immediately after the main shock—even before the warning. Okushiri clearly demonstrated that the impact of tsunamis can be reduced. This event has also become the best-documented tsunami disaster in history. Detailed damage assessments of transportation and telecommunications networks, interviews with survivors and local officials, run-up and inundation measurements, and extensive aerial photography produced a database especially valuable to the U.S.: this urban township is a better analogue of U.S. coastal communities than the other, less developed areas destroyed by tsunamis this decade.

West Coast is the Alaska-Aleutian subduction zone. Included in this region's history of large, tsunami-generating earthquakes are two disasters that drove the establishment of the country's only two tsunami warning centers. The probability of a magnitude 7.4 or greater earthquake occurring somewhere in this zone before 2008 is estimated to be 84 percent.

Another major threat, unrevealed by the written records, lurks off the coasts of Washington State, Oregon and northern California—the Cascadia subduction zone. Brian F. Atwater of the U.S. Geological Survey has identified sand and gravel deposits that he hypothesized were carried inland from the Washington coast by tsunamis born of Cascadia quakes. Recent events support this theory. The Nicaragua tsunami was notable for the amount of sand it transported inland, and researchers have documented similar deposits at inundation sites in Flores, Okushiri, Papua New Guinea and elsewhere.

At least one segment of the Cascadia subduction zone may be approaching the end of a seismic cycle that culminates in an earthquake and destructive tsunami [see "Giant Earthquakes of the Pacific Northwest," by Roy D. Hyndman; SCIENTIFIC AMERICAN, December 1995]. The earthquake danger is believed to be comparable to that in southern California—about a 35 percent probability of occurrence before 2045. Finally, the 1992 Cape Mendocino earthquake and tsunami was a clear reminder that the Cascadia subduction zone can unleash local tsunamis that strike the coast within minutes.

Getting Ready in the U.S.

Hard on the heels of the surprising Cape Mendocino tsunami, the Federal Emergency Management Agency (FEMA) and NOAA funded an earthquake scenario study of northern California and the production of tsunami inundation maps for Eureka and Crescent City in that state. The resulting "all hazards" map was the first of its kind for the U.S. It delineates areas susceptible to tsunami flooding, earthquake-shaking intensity, liquefaction and landslides. Researchers then tackled the possible effects of a great Cascadia subduction zone earthquake and tsunami. About 300,000 people live or work in nearby coastal regions, and at least as many tourists travel through these areas every year. Local tsunami waves could strike communities within minutes of a big quake, leaving little or no time to issue formal warnings. What is more, a Cascadia-born tsunami disaster could cost the region between $1.25 billion and $6.25 billion, a conservative estimate considering the 1993 Okushiri disaster.

Clarification of the threat from the Cascadia subduction zone and the many well-reported tsunami disasters of this decade have stimulated a systematic effort to examine the tsunami hazard in the U.S. In 1997 Congress provided $2.3 million to establish the National Tsunami Hazard Mitigation Program. Alaska, California, Hawaii, Oregon and Washington formed a partnership with NOAA, FEMA and the USGS to tackle the threat of both local- and remote-source tsunamis. The partnership focuses on three interlocking activities: assessing the threat to specific coastal areas; improving early detection of tsunamis and their potential danger; and educating communities to ensure an appropriate response when a tsunami strikes.

The threat to specific coastal areas can be assessed by means of tsunami inundation maps such as those designed for Eureka and Crescent City using state-of-the-art computer modeling. These maps provide critical guidance to local emergency planners charged with identifying evacuation routes. Only Hawaii has systematically developed such maps over the years. To date, three Oregon communities have received maps, six additional maps are in progress in Oregon, Washington and California, and three maps are planned for Alaska.

Rapid, reliable confirmation of the existence of a potentially dangerous tsunami is essential to officials responsible for sounding alarms. Coastal tide gauges have been specially modified to measure tsunamis, and a major upgrade of the seismic network will soon provide more rapid and more complete reports on the nature of the earthquake. These instruments are essential to the warning system, but seismometers measure earthquakes, not tsunamis. And although tide gauges spot tsunamis close to shore, they cannot measure tsunami energy propagating toward a distant coastline. As a consequence, an unacceptable 75 percent false-alarm rate has prevailed since the 1950s. These incidents are expensive, undermine the credibility of the warning system, and place citizens at risk during the evacuation. A false alarm that triggered the evacuation of Honolulu on May 7, 1986, cost Hawaii more than $30 million in lost salaries and business revenues.

NOAA is therefore developing a network of six deep-ocean reporting stations that can track tsunamis and report them in real time, a project known as Deep-Ocean Assessment and Reporting of Tsunamis (DART). Scientists have completed testing of prototype systems and expect the network to be operating reliably in two years. The rationale for this type of warning system is simple: if an earthquake strikes off the coast of Alaska while you're lying on a Hawaiian beach, what you really want to have between you and the quake's epicenter is a DART system. Here's why:

Seismometers staked out around the Pacific Rim can almost instantly pinpoint a big Alaskan quake's location. In the next moment, complex computer programs can predict how long a triggered tsunami would take to reach Hawaii, even though there is not yet evidence a wave exists. After some minutes, tide gauges scattered along the coastlines may detect a tsunami. But the only way to be sure whether a dangerous wave is headed toward a distant coast is to place tsunami detectors in its path and track it across the open ocean.

Conceptually, the idea of such a real-time reporting network is straightforward; however, formidable technological and logistical challenges have held up implementation until now. The DART systems depend on bottom pressure recorders that Hugh B. Milburn, Alex Nakamura, Eddie N. Bernard and I have been perfecting over the past decade at the Pacific Marine Environmental Laboratory. As the crest of a tsunami wave passes by, the bottom recorder detects the increased pressure from the additional volume of overlying water. Even 6,000 meters deep, the sensitive instrument can detect a tsunami no higher than a single centimeter. Ship and storm waves are not detected, because their length is short and, as with currents, changes in pressure are not transmitted all the way to the ocean bottom. We placed the first recorders on the north Pacific seafloor in 1986 and have been using them to record tsunamis ever since. The records cannot be accessed, however, until the instruments are retrieved.

Not the First, Not the Last

EAST ALEUTIAN ISLANDS
April 1, 1946
Maximum wave height: 35 meters
Fatalities: 165

A rash of tsunamis has struck the Pacific Rim this decade, but destructive waves have made their mark long before now. Earthquakes along a seismic subduction zone off Alaska's Aleutian Islands have stirred up the worst tsunamis in U.S. recorded history. On April 1, 1946, a magnitude 7.8 earthquake generated a tsunami that wiped out the Scotch Cap Lighthouse in Alaska and killed five Coast Guard employees. The same tsunami also made a surprise attack five hours later on residents of Hilo, Hawaii. There debris-laden waves up to eight meters high caught a number of school-children before classes began and wiped out a hospital. Altogether the killer waves took the lives of 165 people, 159 of them in Hawaii, and caused more than $26 million in damage.

The U.S. reacted to this disaster by setting up the Pacific Tsunami Warning Center in Hawaii in 1948. Similarly, three years after the March 28, 1964, Alaskan tsunami that took more than 100 lives, the Alaska Regional Tsunami Warning System (now the West Coast and Alaska Tsunami Warning Center) was established. Today a newly recognized threat from a seismic zone off the West Coast has driven the U.S. to take action against a tsunami disaster *before* it occurs. This endeavor by state and federal partners features a systematic tsunami inundation mapping program, a state-of-the-art, deep-ocean tsunami detection network and educational campaigns to prepare coastal communities for a potential disaster.

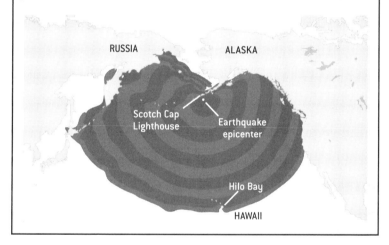

Ideally, when the bottom recorders detect a tsunami, acoustic chirps will transmit the measurements to a car-size buoy at the ocean surface, which will then relay the information to a ground station via satellite. The surface buoy systems, the satellite relay technology and the bottom recorders have proved themselves at numerous deep-ocean stations, including an array of 70 weather buoys set up along the equator to track El Niño, the oceanographic phenomenon so infamous for its effect on world climate. The biggest challenge has been developing a reliable acoustic transmission system. Over the past three years, four prototype DART systems have been deployed, worked for a time, then failed. Design improvements to a second-generation system have refined communication between the bottom recorders and the buoys.

In the next two years, our laboratory plans to establish five stations spread across the north Pacific from the west Aleutians to Oregon and a sixth sited on

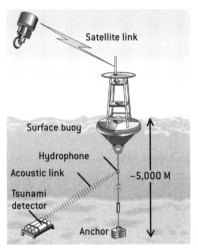

Deep-ocean tsunami detectors (*left*) and a major upgrade of existing earthquake monitoring networks (*triangles on map*)—both scheduled for installation within two years—lead the U.S. effort to take the surprise out of tsunami attacks. The deep-ocean detectors depend on high-tech sensors stationed on the seafloor. When one of these instruments senses a tsunami wave overhead, it will send acoustic signals to a buoy at the surface, which will then relay the warning via satellite to the officials who are responsible for sounding an alarm.

the equator to intercept tsunamis generated off South America. More buoys would reduce the possibility that tsunami waves might sneak between them, but the current budget limits the number that NOAA can afford. This is where detailed computer simulations become invaluable. Combined with the buoy measurements, the simulations will provide more accurate predictions to guide officials who may have only a few minutes to decide whether to sound an alarm.

Even the most reliable warning is ineffective if people do not respond appropriately. Community education is thus perhaps the most important aspect of the national mitigation program's threefold mission. Each state is identifying coordinators who will provide information and guidance to community emergency managers during tsunami disasters. Interstate coordination is also crucial to public safety because U.S. citizens are highly mobile, and procedures must be compatible from state to state. Standard tsunami signage has already been put in place along many coastlines.

Tsunami researchers and emergency response officials agree that future destructive tsunamis are inevitable and technology alone cannot save lives. Coastal inhabitants must be able to recognize the signs of a possible tsunami—such as strong, prolonged ground shaking—and know that they should seek higher ground immediately. Coastal communities need inundation maps that identify far in advance what areas are likely to be flooded so that they can lay out evacuation routes. The proactive enterprise now under way in the U.S. will surely upgrade tsunami prediction for a much larger region of the Pacific. All of these efforts are essential to the over-riding goal of avoiding tragedies such as those in Papua New Guinea, Nicaragua and elsewhere.

The Author

Frank I. González is Tsunami Research Program Leader and Director of the Center for Tsunami Inundation Mapping Efforts at NOAA's Pacific Marine Environmental Laboratory in Seattle. He earned his Ph.D. in physical oceanography from the University of Hawaii in 1975 and joined the laboratory two years later. In 1984 he received NOAA's highest award for outstanding scientific research—the NOAA Administrator's Award—for his work on hazardous ocean waves. He has participated in field surveys and documentation of three devastating tsunamis that recently occurred in Nicaragua, Indonesia and Japan. The author dedicates this article to the memory of his wife, Yolanda Cano González. In his words: "Yolanda was well known by many in the tsunami research community. She was a gifted, award-winning teacher who loved children, gardening, science and, wondrously, me. As she loved and nurtured her gardens, Yolanda loved and nurtured her students and their enthusiasm for science."

On December 26, 2004, more than 175,000 people lost their lives in one of the world's worst natural disasters. Possibly millions of people in Southeast Asia, South Asia, and East Africa suffered personal injury or property loss because of the 2004 tsunami. This next article presents a particularly compelling description of the event because it was written just after it happened by a reporter working in India very near the tsunami's point of origin.

As you have already read, earthquakes can affect other natural systems, like those that fuel volcanoes. Now you will learn how earthquakes can influence water movement. A tsunami is a series of huge ocean waves that may build upon each other to result in a massive wall of water. Hours before the 2004 tsunami struck, an earthquake measuring 9.0 crashed two undersea plates together with enough force to lift the seafloor. The earthquake itself, which happened twenty miles below the ocean's surface, was scary. Most undersea earthquakes, however, do not result in devastating tsunamis. Despite reports of the earthquake, most locals and vacationers did not change their plans. In fact, many survivors reported that they were enjoying a pleasant morning on the beach when the tsunami approached. The reporter also documents a number of changes to the shape and rotation of the earth as a consequence of the earthquake. —JV

"The Scarred Earth"
by **Madhusree Mukerjee**
Scientific American, **March 2005**

A year of death and destruction wreaked mostly by
humans ended with nature flexing her own muscles, to
terrifying effect. A section of the earth's crust hundreds
of kilometers long tore off its moorings, slamming into
the seawater above. The resulting tsunami traveled at
700 kilometers per hour to rear up like a hydra onto
shores, sweeping away some 225,000 lives and millions
of livelihoods across 12 nations. Now, as broken-hearted
survivors turn to piecing together the remnants, scientists are scrutinizing the oceanic and island terrain to
determine how the crust has changed and to gauge
what further horrors the earth may have in store.

The magnitude 9.0 earthquake was the largest
ever recorded in the region and the world's biggest
since a 1964 Alaskan quake. The underground tear
started 100 kilometers off the coast of Sumatra, on the
western edge of the Burma plate. This "sliver" plate,
a long, thin section of crust that reaches southward
from Myanmar (Burma), pushes over and against the
India plate to its west at the rate of 14 millimeters a
year; on December 26, 2004, the Burma plate jerked
westward and upward along an incline by perhaps
15 meters.

According to an early reconstruction by seismologist
Chen Ji of the California Institute of Technology, the
earthquake initially displaced 400 kilometers of crust

20 kilometers below the seabed. The tear very likely continued farther north but too slowly to generate seismic waves. (Long ruptures produce very low frequency seismic waves that are difficult to measure and interpret.) "Our preliminary tsunami modeling indicates the length of the rupture was significantly larger than the estimates the seismologists are putting up," remarks Frank Gonzalez of the National Oceanic and Atmospheric Administration in Seattle. In any case, the earthquake shook the bottom of the sea along a ridge aligned north to south, sending upraised walls of water barreling mainly east and west.

On reaching gently sloping coastlines the tsunami slowed down, shoaled and rose many meters to descend on unsuspecting humans. It first bulldozed

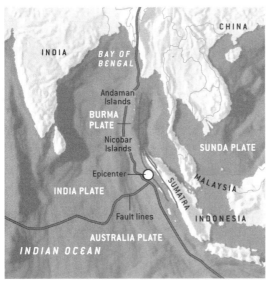

Colliding plates: The Burma tectonic plate lurched west over the India plate, uplifting the seafloor and triggering the December 26, 2004, tsunami.

coastal towns in Sumatra and, farther north, washed clean, over several of the Nicobar Islands, leaving in places only a handful of survivors clinging to treetops. Sloshing within the confines of the Andaman Sea to the east, it carried off vacationers in Thailand. The westward wave traveled across the Indian Ocean as swiftly as a jet plane, striking India and Sri Lanka. Six hours later it claimed lives on Africa's shores and kept on going until it had circled the globe and dissipated.

At the same time the tsunami scoured the planet, the earthquake permanently altered its shape. Because the plates pulled tight and snug over one another, the earth's crust became more compact. Calculations suggest that, like an ice skater drawing in her arms, the contraction made the planet rotate faster, by perhaps three microseconds. And because the ocean bottom near the epicenter thrust upward, the planet's water now has less room, causing the sea level to rise by about a millimeter.

More locally, the earthquake and its aftershocks changed the shape and orientation of virtually the entire Burma plate and the lands it supports—in particular, the Andaman and Nicobar islands. The two island groups are the peaks of an undersea mountain range, raised by the scraping up of soft sediments as the plate's leading edge pressed down and forward against the India plate. After the earthquake, some of the Nicobar Islands seem to have sunk, and one island, Trinkat, has split into three pieces, with fish now swimming around once idyllic, palm-fringed villages.

When Old Ways Trump New Ways

Days after the tsunami, an Indian coast guard helicopter flew 50 kilometers west of the town of Port Blair in the Andaman Islands. There, hovering over North Sentinel Island, it found itself targeted by two-meter-long arrows: evidently the inhabitants had survived. The Sentinelese are Paleolithic hunter-gatherers who choose to live in isolation, they are one of four groups of Andaman aboriginals, all 500 or so of whom appear to have run to high ground after they felt the earthquake.

"Our forefathers told us," explains one tribesman, "that when the earth shakes, the sea will rise up onto the land. They said we should run to the hills or get into a boat and go far out to sea." The Andamanese had a lead time of less than an hour. So while people in the information age groped through phone books to issue a tsunami warning that never arrived, those in the Stone Age had packed up their children, baskets, nets, bows, arrows and embers and run for the hills.

The western edge of the Burma plate has risen a few meters—exposing coral beds around the tiny island of North Sentinel—whereas the eastern edge has dropped. According to Survey of India, a government mapping department, the main town in the Andaman-Nicobar region, Port Blair, has shifted by a meter and sunk by 25 centimeters. Such tilting is to be expected, notes Joseph Curray of the Scripps Institution of

Oceanography in La Jolla, Calif.: one undersea ridge south of the Nicobars was once, he suspects, a piece of Sumatra that sunk in the distant past. "Sooner or later Banda Aceh will subside" and disappear into the ocean, he concludes of the Sumatran city.

"Sooner" for a geologist usually means "later" for other humans: the earthquake and its aftershocks, Curray believes, eventually ruptured and released stress along the entire western edge of the Burma plate, making other massive jolts unlikely for a century. Large quakes could still be expected along the eastern edge, he warns: the Burma plate, drifting northward around 25 millimeters a year, tends to stick and unstick against the plate to its east in motions that produce "strike-slip" earthquakes. Such earthquakes probably would not result in tsunamis, because they would cause the water column above mainly to shear, not to lift.

But Kerry Sieh of Caltech suspects that an increased risk of a tsunami-spawning earthquake prevails south of the epicenter, where the rupture did not propagate. Sensitive measurements of the region's contours will be necessary to resolve this question.

Seismometers, tide gauges and other detection instruments now being deployed will make the next tsunami, if not the next earthquake, come as less of a surprise. Still, the coastal areas of Asia face future challenges: cyclones and their attendant surges will take an increasing toll as global warming disturbs weather systems. The devastated communities should ideally be rebuilt on high ground far from shore, where they would be protected by mangroves from the ever rising ocean. But for millions of the poor in crowded countries, such safety may never be possible.

Madhusree Mukerjee, reporting from Kolkata, India, is author of The Land of Naked People: Encounters with Stone Age Islanders, *a book about the Andamanese.*

Science writers, like political experts, often express a viewpoint in their stories. Earlier in this volume, for example, geologist Peter Cervelli presented his theory on how researchers might be able to predict earthquakes based on known tremblers. In the following article, Sarah Simpson presents a different point of view. She discusses a study that appeared in a peer-reviewed journal. She also addresses the media coverage it received.

The original study mentioned that landslides could trigger tsunamis and that such events could occur offshore of very highly populated areas in the United States. Specifically, the deep sea off the coasts of North Carolina and New Jersey appears to be vulnerable to underwater landslides due to seafloor instability and "gas blowouts," or areas where natural gas collects and can lead to explosive pressure. Some media at the time used

*the information to suggest that a tsunami could
hit the eastern United States.*

*Simpson agrees but thinks the possibility of
a tsunami striking North Carolina and New
Jersey is remote. Given her summary of the May
2000 Geology study, what do you think? Should
we worry even if chances for disaster are slim, or
is it better to be safe than sorry? These are the
kinds of questions that politicians and scientists
often must grapple with when deciding what to
study and where to allocate funds. —JV*

"Killer Waves on the East Coast?"
by Sarah Simpson
Scientific American, October 2000

If you perused any of several metropolitan newspapers
along the Eastern seaboard this summer, you might
have imagined a disaster of hurricane proportions
striking the coast on a clear, blue day. With a sudden
crumbling of the seafloor, the Atlantic Ocean would
rise up and flatten Virginia Beach and Cape Hatteras.
Giant waves might even surge up the Potomac River
and flood the U.S. capital.

The notion of a tsunami striking the mid-Atlantic
coast is startling—those disasters tend to hit earthquake-
prone locales of the Pacific Rim, where land slipping
along underwater faults sloshes the sea into threatening
swells. But despite the breathless news reports, a long
string of ifs and buts stretches between an imminent

threat of an East Coast tsunami and its newly discovered potential cause: underwater landslides.

The landslide concern stems from new indications of looming instability atop the slope between the shallow continental shelf and the deep sea, off the coasts of North Carolina and New Jersey. Enormous cracks northeast of Cape Hatteras could be an underwater landslide in the making, three scientists suggested in the May *Geology*. Mud suddenly breaking loose and tearing downslope could displace enough water to swamp the nearby coastline with tsunami waves some five meters (15 feet) high—an event comparable to the storm surges of Hurricane Fran, which ravaged North Carolina in 1996.

The day after the media caught wind of the report, television helicopters were landing on the lawn of the Woods Hole Oceanographic Institution in Massachusetts, the workplace of the report's lead author, Neal W. Driscoll. Elsewhere, Driscoll's colleagues Jeffrey K. Weissel of Columbia University's Lamont-Doherty Earth Observatory and John A. Goff of the University of Texas at Austin were also fielding calls from eager reporters. "We underestimated the excitement the paper would cause," Weissel says.

What the scientists knew—and what many news accounts failed to emphasize—was that although a tsunami would be devastating, the potential risk was remarkably unclear. At the time, the researchers had no idea when a landslide might occur (if ever), no mathematical predictions of the waves that might be generated and no evidence of a tsunami ever having struck the mid-Atlantic coast in the past. Still, Weissel maintains that "the paper would have been incomplete without a portion on tsunamis." At the heart of the scientists' concern is the growing evidence that underwater landslides—not earthquakes alone—pose a tsunami threat [see "Tsunami!," by Frank I. González, SCIENTIFIC AMERICAN, May 1999].

Oceanographers conducted the first intensive investigation of this theory after the 1998 Papua New Guinea tsunami. At least 2,200 people died—drowned, impaled on mangrove branches or bludgeoned by debris—when waves up to 15 meters high struck the country's north coast. A magnitude-7.1 earthquake had rocked the area only minutes before, but the waves were up to five times larger than expected for a quake that size. When oceanographers inspected the nearby seafloor, they found evidence of a landslide that could have enlarged the tsunami.

Two rare landslides in the western Atlantic also fuel the tsunami concern. In 1929 an earthquake-triggered landslide off Newfoundland's Grand Banks spawned a tsunami that killed 51 people. A similarly massive slide occurred some 20,000 years ago just to the south of the cracks discovered off the North Carolina coast.

Had scientists detected those cracks 10 years earlier, before underwater landslides were a suspected cause of tsunamis, their interpretations might have been different, Weissel says. But in light of this new historical

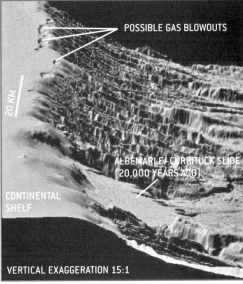

Giant gas blowouts, which may have cratered the seafloor off the North Carolina coast, could presage underwater slides. Potential blowouts (not shown) also lie off New Jersey.

evidence, his team couldn't ignore the possibility. Frank I. González, leader of the National Oceanic and Atmospheric Administration's tsunami research program in Seattle, agrees: "I think these guys were right on to call attention to the potential tsunami risk."

Based on sonar images, the cracks have turned out to be giant craters—some five kilometers long and two kilometers across—that the team now thinks formed from eruptions of gas trapped in the sediments. What's more, additional gas is still waiting to blow. The researchers don't know when the past blowouts occurred, but they have reason to think they could have been explosive: such eruptions have destroyed oil rigs that penetrated gas deposits in the Gulf of Mexico and the North Sea.

In the July 14 *Science*, a second team reported another potential cause of seafloor blowouts. Peter B. Flemings and Brandon Dugan of Pennsylvania State University noted that explosions of waterlogged sediments could have carved several mysterious submarine canyons about 150 kilometers east of Atlantic City, N.J.

During an Ocean Drilling Program research cruise in 1997, Flemings and the crew drilled into one-million-year-old mud that contained up to 65 percent water. The soggy sediments were buried so fast that the water had nowhere to go. But the pressure caused by being buried 600 meters below the seafloor means that deep erosion could unleash the water with a bang. Flemings and Dugan didn't mention tsunamis in their journal article, but the media didn't miss the connection. "I just continually remind people that we haven't done any work on whether a tsunami would be generated," Dugan says.

Such a prediction would be difficult to make, anyway. It takes a sudden flow of a large volume of mud to create a tsunami; the scientists don't know whether the canyons formed quickly—in one explosive event—or eroded over tens of thousands of years. Even today, muddy seeps and geysers bleed off trapped water little by little.

Nor is it clear whether gas blowouts farther south would stabilize the slope by reducing the pressurized gas or destabilize it by rendering the shelf edge more precariously balanced than before, Weissel says. The fact is that landslides may never occur in either region. And until scientists can estimate the frequency of landslides—whatever the cause—it will be impossible to calculate the probability of a future tsunami. From Dugan's perspective, the bottom line is this: "Are these blowouts preventable? No. Should people be worried? No."

2 Volcanic Eruptions and Other Geological Events

The following article focuses on a specific volcano in Italy. Similar to the way the "Tsunami!" article presented information that researchers may apply to all tsunamis, "Mount Etna's Ferocious Future" also provides a thorough overview of volcanoes in general. According to author Tom Pfeiffer, three basic kinds of volcanoes exist in the world. Mount Etna, however, does not seem to fit well into any of the described categories.

Italy's geology has changed enormously over millions of years as the earth's plates moved and tectonic faults developed. While volcanoes evolve over such extended periods, they can unleash a violent fury in mere minutes, as the author learned when he and a group of observers witnessed an eruption at a distance that was too close for comfort.

Scientists do not yet fully understand how and why volcanoes erupt, but as Pfeiffer discusses, analysis of the magma, or molten rock, that volcanoes release can provide some clues. In Italy, locals probably hope answers will be revealed soon, as Mount Etna's activity has been increasing in recent decades. —JV

"Mount Etna's Ferocious Future"
by Tom Pfeiffer
Translated by Alexander R. McBirney
Scientific American, April 2003

Last October about 1,000 Italians fled their homes after Mount Etna, the famous volcano on the island of Sicily, rumbled to life. Shooting molten rock more than 500 meters into the air, Etna sent streams of lava rushing down its northeastern and southern flanks. The eruption was accompanied by hundreds of earth-quakes measuring up to 4.3 on the Richter scale. As a huge plume of smoke and ash drifted across the Mediterranean Sea, residents of Linguaglossa (the name means "tongues" of lava) tried to ward off the lava flows by parading a statue of their patron saint through the town's streets.

Perhaps because of divine intervention, nobody was hurt and damage was not widespread. But the episode was unnerving because it was so similar to an erratic eruption on the volcano's southern flank in the summer of 2001 that destroyed parts of a tourist complex and threatened the town of Nicolosi. Some of the lavas discharged in both events were of an unusual type last produced in large amounts at the site about 15,000 years ago. At that time, a series of catastrophic eruptions led to the collapse of one of Etna's predecessor volcanoes.

The Sicilians living near Mount Etna have long regarded the volcano as a restless but relatively friendly neighbor. Though persistently active, Etna has not had a major explosive eruption—such as the devastating 1980 event at Mount Saint Helens in Washington State—for hundreds of years. But now some researchers believe they have found evidence that Etna is very gradually becoming more dangerous. It is unlikely that Etna will explode like Mount Saint Helens in the near future, but fierce eruptions may become more common.

Mountains of Fire

The name "Etna" is derived from an old Indo-Germanic root meaning "burned" or "burning." Extensive reports and legends record about 3,000 years of the volcano's activity, but a reliable chronicle has been available only since the 17th century. Most of the earlier accounts are limited to particularly violent eruptions, such as those occurring in 122 BC and AD 1169, 1329, 1536 and 1669. During the eruption in 1669, an enormous lava flow buried part of the city of Catania before pouring into the sea.

With a surface area of approximately 1,200 square kilometers, Etna is Europe's largest volcano. Its 3,340-meter-high peak is often covered with snow. Only the upper 2,000 meters consists of volcanic material; the mountain rests on a base of sedimentary rock beds. Blocks of this material are occasionally caught in the magma—the molten rock moving upward—and ejected at the surface. Numerous blocks of white sandstone were blown out during the 2001 and 2002 eruptions. This phenomenon occurs whenever magma must open new paths for its ascent, as is usually the case with lateral eruptions (those that occur on the volcano's flanks).

The volcano is more than 500,000 years old. Remnants of its earliest eruptions are still preserved in nearby coastal regions in the form of pillow lavas, which emerge underwater and do in fact look like giant pillows. At first, a shield volcano—so called because it resembles a shield placed face-up on the ground—grew in a depression in the area where Etna now stands. Today a much steeper cone rests on the ancient shield volcano. It consists of at least five generations of volcanic edifices that have piled up during the past 100,000 to 200,000 years, each atop the remnants of its eroded or partly collapsed predecessor. The present-day cone has been built in the past 5,000 to 8,000 years. Among Etna's special features are the hundreds of small cinder cones scattered about its flanks. Each marks a lateral outbreak of magma. One of the world's most productive volcanoes, Etna has spewed about 30 million cubic meters of igneous material each year since 1970, with a peak eruption rate of 300 cubic meters a second.

Etna is also one of the most puzzling volcanoes. Why has the magma that produced it risen to the surface at this particular spot, and why does it continue to do so in such large quantities? The answers should be found in the theory of plate tectonics, which posits that the earth's outermost shell consists of about a dozen vast plates, each between about five and 150 kilometers thick. The plates constitute the planet's crust and the uppermost part of the mantle. Like pieces of ice floating on the ocean, these plates drift independently, sometimes moving apart and at other times colliding. The 530 active volcanoes of the world are divided into three major types according to their positions on or between these plates.

The first and most numerous type is found along the rift zones, where two plates are moving apart. The best examples are the long midocean ridges. Forces beneath the plates rip them apart along a fracture, and the separation causes an upwelling of hotter material from the underlying mantle. This material melts as it rises, producing basalt (the most common kind of magma), which contains large amounts of iron and magnesium. The basaltic melt fills the space created by the separating plates, thus continuously adding new oceanic crust.

The second type is located along the subduction zones, where two plates converge. Normally, a colder and heavier oceanic plate dives below a continental plate. The process that leads to the formation of magma in this environment is completely different: water and other fluids entrained with the sinking plate are released under increasing pressure and temperature, mainly at depths of about 100 kilometers. These fluids rise into the overlying, hotter mantle wedge and lower the melting temperature of the rocks. The resulting magmas, which are more viscous and gas-rich than the basaltic melts of the rift zones, contain less iron and magnesium and more silica and volatile components (mainly water and carbon dioxide).

These factors make the volcanoes in subduction zones far more menacing than volcanoes in rift zones. Because the viscous, gas-rich magma does not flow easily out of the earth, pressure builds up until the molten rock is ejected explosively. The sudden release of gases fragments the magma into volcanic projectiles, including bombs (rounded masses of lava), lapilli (small stony or glassy pieces) and ash. Such volcanoes typically have steep cones composed of alternating layers of loose airborne deposits and lava flows. Some of the best-known examples of subduction-zone volcanoes rise along the margins of the Pacific Ocean and in the island arcs. This Ring of Fire includes Mount Saint Helens, Unzen in Japan and Pinatubo in the Philippines, all of which have erupted in the past three decades.

The third type of volcano develops independently of the movements of the tectonic plates and is found above hot spots caused by mantle plumes, currents of unusually hot material that ascend by thermal convection from deep in the earth's mantle. As the mantle plumes approach the surface, decreasing pressure causes them to produce melts that bore their way through the crust, creating a chain of hotspot volcanoes. Most hot-spot volcanoes produce highly fluid lava flows that build large, flat shield volcanoes, such as Mauna Loa in Hawaii.

At the Crossroads

Etna, however, cannot be assigned to any of the three
principal categories of volcanoes. It is located in a
geologically complex area, which owes its current form
to tectonic processes that have been active for the past
50 million to 60 million years. An ocean basin that
formerly existed between Eurasia and the northward-
moving African continent was swallowed to a large
extent by the Eurasian plate. About 100 million
years ago two smaller plates, Iberia and Adria, split
off from the Eurasian and African plates because of
enormous shearing stresses related to the separation of
North America from Eurasia (and the opening of the
Atlantic Ocean).

Mountain belts arose along the fronts where the
plates collided. Italy's Apennines developed when the
Iberian and Adriatic plates met. During this process,
the Italian peninsula was rotated counterclockwise by
as much as 120 degrees to its current position. Today
Etna is situated close to the junction of the African,
Eurasian and Adriatic plates. Individual blocks from
these plates have been superimposed and welded
together on Sicily. Major tectonic faults cross the
area around the volcano as a result of intense regional
stresses within the crust.

For a long time researchers believed that Etna's
position at the crossroads of these faults was the
explanation for its volcanism. The presence of faults,
however, accounts only for the ability of magma to

reach the surface; it does not explain why the magma is produced in the first place. According to most theories, the prevailing forces in the Sicilian crust are similar to those in rift zones—extensional stresses that cause thinning of the crust and upwelling of the underlying mantle. But at Sicily the African and Eurasian plates are colliding, so one would expect the stresses to be compressive rather than extensional. Moreover, only about 20 percent of the magma erupted at Etna has a chemical composition similar to that of a rift-zone volcano.

Judging from its magma and pattern of activity, Etna is most similar to hotspot volcanoes such as those in Hawaii. Recent theories suggest that it has developed above an active mantle plume, but no direct evidence for this plume has been detected. So far scientists have been unable to explain all the characteristics of this enigmatic volcano. For example, Etna is one of the few volcanoes in which magma is almost continuously rising. Its active periods can last for years or even decades and are interrupted only by short intervals of quietness. This pattern implies the existence of two things: first, a constant flow of magma from the mantle to the deep and shallow magma reservoirs beneath the volcano and, second, an open conduit through which magma can rise. In fact, the conduits between Etna's magma chambers and the summit craters seem to be very long lived structures. Seismic investigations have shown that the rising magma produces little noise and appears to move rather smoothly, without encountering major obstacles.

The kind of activity that prevails at Etna depends primarily on the level of magma inside its conduits. The low pressure in the upper part of the magma column allows the dissolved gases (mainly water and carbon dioxide) to escape. The resulting bubbles rise within the magma column and pop at the surface, throwing out liquid and solid fragments. When the level of the magma column is fairly deep inside the volcano, only gases and fine ash particles reach the crater rim. When it is closer to the surface, larger fragments (lapilli and bombs) are thrown out as well. In the rare cases when the magma column itself reaches the crater rim, the degassing magma pours over the rim or through a crack and forms a lava flow.

Besides lava flows, Etna produces an almost constant, rhythmic discharge of steam, ash and molten rock. Known as a strombolian eruption (named after Stromboli, a volcano on one of the Aeolian Islands about 100 kilometers north of Etna), this activity sometimes culminates in violent lava fountains jetting hundreds of meters into the air. During the spectacular series of eruptions at Etna's southeast crater in the first half of 2000, these fountains rose as high as 1,200 meters above the crater's rim—a stunning height rarely observed at any volcano.

To witness such an eruption from close range can be extremely dangerous, as I have learned from experience. In February 2000, violent eruptions at Etna's southeast crater were occurring at 12- or 24-hour intervals. On the evening of February 15, while

I was observing the crater from about 800 meters away with a group of spectators, a white cloud of steam rose from the crater's mouth. It rapidly became thicker and denser. After a few minutes, the first red spots began dancing above the crater, rising and falling back into it. The explosions grew stronger, first slowly, then with breathtaking speed, throwing bombs more than 1,000 meters above the rim. Soon the volcanic cone surrounding the crater was covered with glowing rocks. At the same time, a fountain of lava started to rise from a fracture on the flank of the cone. Several other fountains rose from the crater and formed a roaring, golden curtain that illuminated the scene like daylight. Some larger bombs crashed into the snow not far from us, but we felt secure in our viewing position. The fountain was nearly vertical, and a strong wind carried the mass of glowing lapilli and ash gently away from us.

Suddenly the lava fountain changed direction, sending a lateral outburst straight toward us. Just in time we reached the shelter of an abandoned mountain hut with a thick concrete roof. A heavy rain of incandescent stones fell around us; lava bombs of all sizes tumbled down, spraying thousands of sparks. Fortunately, our shelter was not hit by anything large, although a two-meter-wide bomb plunged into the snow nearby. After an endless two minutes, the lava fountain rose vertically again and stayed in this position for another 10 minutes. Then its supply of magma from below seemed to be exhausted. The fountain collapsed as if it were sucked back into the crater. The entire spectacle was finished 30 minutes after it began. In front of us, the 300-meter-high cone still glowed red but was completely silent.

Natural Air Polluter

Etna's reputation as a relatively friendly volcano stems mainly from the fact that its lavas are very fluid. Such lavas are easily ejected to the surface, unlike the viscous magmas produced by subduction-zone volcanoes. But Etna's magmas also contain a great amount of gas, which can make eruptions much more explosive. During a particularly violent phase, Etna expels up to 20,000 tons of sulfur dioxide a day, making the volcano one of nature's worst air polluters. The high sulfur content of Etna's magma is hard to understand; this characteristic is more typical of subduction-zone volcanoes than of basaltic volcanoes.

What is more, Etna's composition indicates that the volcano has indeed experienced major explosive eruptions similar in size to those of Pinatubo in 1991 and Mount Saint Helens in 1980. Etna's last big explosion appears to have occurred in 122 BC. During that event, more than one cubic kilometer of basaltic lava erupted in a giant column loaded with lapilli and ash. Deposits formed by this eruption are up to two meters thick on Etna's upper slopes and are still exposed in some areas. In Catania, about 30 kilometers from the summit, the deposits are between 10 and 25 centimeters thick. If such an event were to occur today, it would be a disaster. The roofs of many houses in the area would collapse from the weight of the ash.

The unusual flank eruptions of 2001 and 2002 made it clear that Etna is not tame. In 2001 as many as five fractures opened on both sides of the mountain, through which huge masses of lava started to pour. A new crater was born at an elevation of 2,500 meters. Extremely active, it spewed lava fountains and dense clouds of ash, growing within a few days to a cone about 100 meters high. Especially spectacular were the giant magma bubbles that rose within the new crater and detonated with awesome power. Even at a distance of several kilometers, the force of the explosions rattled doors and windows.

Researchers soon determined that two distinct eruptions were occurring simultaneously. The opening of the fractures near Etna's summit (between 2,700 and 3,000 meters above sea level) was a continuation of the volcanic activity that had been roiling the summit craters for years. But the eruptions at the lower fractures (at elevations between 2,100 and 2,500 meters) produced a more evolved type of magma that obviously had rested for a prolonged period in a separate chamber, where it could change its chemical composition. (A similar pattern was also evident in the 2002 eruptions.) This second kind of magma included centimeter-size crystals of the mineral amphibole, which is very rarely found in Etna's lavas. Besides iron, magnesium and silica, amphibole incorporates water in its crystal structure. The mineral can form only from a magma that contains sufficient amounts of water. Obviously, two different plumbing systems of the volcano were active at the same time: one associated with the central, more or less constantly active conduit and the other with an independent conduit off to the side.

The magmas ejected through this second conduit were last produced in large quantities at Etna about 15,000 years ago, when devastating eruptions caused the collapse of one of Etna's predecessors, the Ellittico volcano. Is their reappearance a sign that a catastrophic explosive eruption will happen in the near future? The answer depends on where Etna's magmas come from. Identifying their origins can be tricky: analyzing the erupted magma can be misleading, because the chemical composition of the original melt often changes during its ascent through the crust. Geologists have learned, however, that surface lavas sometimes contain crystals that preserve the composition of the original magma. If a crystal begins to form at an early stage in the life of a magma, it may include minuscule droplets of the primitive melt and grow around them. These melt inclusions are thus isolated from all subsequent chemical changes.

Analyzing such melt inclusions, though, is difficult. Until recently, almost no suitable data were available for Etna. In 1996 a French-Italian research team consisting of Pierre Schiano (Blaise Pascal University in France), Roberto Clocchiatti (National Center for Scientific Research in France), Luisa Ottolini (National Research Council in Italy) and Tiziana Busà (then at the

University of Catania in Italy) began a comprehensive investigation of the magmas of Etna and neighboring volcanoes. The researchers looked for glassy inclusions in olivine crystals, which are among the first to form from a primitive melt. The tiny inclusions they discovered, each less than two tenths of a millimeter in diameter, were remelted on a heating plate, then quenched to create a homogeneous glass. The team determined the chemical composition of the inclusions using a microprobe (which directs narrow beams of x-rays at a sample) and a secondary ion mass spectrometer (which employs ion beams).

Changing Character

The scientists paid special attention to the trace elements, such as cesium and barium, which are rare in igneous rocks. When a melt forms deep underground, the trace elements in the source rock migrate almost completely to the magma. Because their relative concentrations remain nearly unchanged, the trace elements offer a geologic fingerprint of the origin of the melt. The magmas that erupted at Etna more than about 100,000 years ago had compositions similar to those from the older, now extinct volcanoes of the Iblean Mountains in southern Sicily. The trace-element patterns were also close to those found in magmas from hotspot volcanoes in Hawaii and the Azores. The early volcanism at Etna was apparently fueled by a mantle plume, probably the same one that fed the Iblean volcanoes about 100 kilometers to the south.

But the analysis of the younger magmas (those that have been expelled within the past 100,000 years) revealed a much different picture. They have large concentrations of trace elements such as cesium, potassium, rubidium and barium, but they appeared to be depleted of elements such as titanium and zirconium. Remarkably similar patterns are found at the Aeolian Island volcanoes, which include Stromboli and Vulcano. This island arc most likely owes its existence to tectonic forces—specifically, the subduction of oceanic crust from the Ionian Sea under the Calabrian block (the southernmost part of the Italian mainland). Schiano and Clocchiatti are convinced that the similarity of the magmas is no coincidence. They believe that Etna has two sources of magma: the mantle plume that gave birth to the volcano and a second component that is identical to the magma feeding the Aeolian volcanoes. Furthermore, Etna's youngest magmas have the greatest amounts of this second component.

How does Etna produce its fiery mix of magmas? One possibility is that the two magmas form at different locations and mix somewhere within Ema's plumbing system. This hypothesis would imply that the magma below the Aeolian Islands travels more than 100 kilo-meters along a tectonic fault to Etna. It is considered highly unlikely, though, that such an underground magma passage exists. Researchers think it is more probable that the two magma *sources* are mixing. According to this model, part of the subducted slab of the Ionian plate has slowly migrated southward and come within reach of the plume beneath Etna. When the rising plume passes by the edge of the sinking slab, it creates the mix of magmas that emerges from the volcano.

Etna's activity has increased markedly since 1970, with more frequent eruptions and more volcanic material ejected. Researchers cannot be certain, however, whether this upsurge is caused by tectonic forces or by a fresh batch of magma rising from the mantle. If Etna is indeed transforming into an explosive subduction-zone volcano, the process will be a gradual one. As Schiano and Clocchiatti emphasize, "The observed change [from a hot-spot toward an island-arc volcano] is taking place in geological time and not in a human lifetime." Thus, Etna is unlikely to experience a catastrophic explosive eruption soon.

But if the researchers' hypothesis is correct, Etna's eruptions will grow increasingly violent. Some tens of thousands of years from now, Etna may well become as dangerous as Mount Saint Helens or Pinatubo. Fortunately, the Sicilians should have plenty of time to adapt to the new situation.

The Author

Tom Pfeiffer has become very familiar with Mount Etna, photographing many of the volcano's recent eruptions. He is a Ph.D. student in the department of earth sciences at the University of Århus in Denmark. Pfeiffer has done research at the Hawaiian Volcano Observatory at Kilauea volcano and the Vesuvius Observatory in Naples.

His dissertation is about the Minoan eruption on the Greek island of Santorini that devastated the eastern Mediterranean region around 1645 BC. An earlier version of this article appeared in the May 2002 issue of Spektrum der Wissenschaft, Scientific American's *sister publication in Germany.*

In addition to studying the chemicals found within magma released by volcanoes, geologists also are analyzing the gas emitted by the imposing mounts. The article is entitled "Volcanic Sniffing," but few scientists would want to risk standing on the edge of a volcano to take a whiff. Instead, they are developing high-tech equipment to "sniff," or detect, the chemical components of volcanic gas and lava. We now are at the stage where such detection can occur on the molecular level.

Choi describes a method involving lasers, which are devices that utilize the natural oscillations of atoms or molecules between energy levels to generate electromagnetic radiation within the visible or invisible spectra of light. Lasers sweep across volcano sites, and scientists can operate them from a safe distance. The lasers allow the researchers to look for changes in carbon isotopes. Isotopes are classes of atoms that are similar to chemical elements *(such as carbon, tin, or hydrogen) but whose mass and physical properties differ from those elements. Carbon isotopes deteriorate over very long periods, so scientists use them to date archaeological objects. In terms of volcanoes, tiny changes to isotopes appear to be linked to rising volcanic activity. —JV*

"Volcanic Sniffing"
by Charles Choi
Scientific American, November 2004

In A.D. 79 Mount Vesuvius erupted, annihilating the cities of Pompeii and Herculaneum and killing thousands who did not evacuate in time. To avert a similar fate for present-day Naples, which lies six miles west of the still active Vesuvius, as well as for the cities near volatile Mount Etna in Sicily, a novel laser system could soon forecast volcanic eruptions up to months in advance.

Current methods to predict eruptions have downsides. Seismometers can monitor tremors and other ground activity that signal a volcano's awakening, but their readings can prove imprecise or complicated to interpret. Scanning for escaping gases can reveal whether magma is moving inside, but the instruments used to analyze such emissions are often too delicate and bulky for life outside a laboratory. "You have to collect samples from the volcano, bring them to a lab, and often wait through backlogs of weeks to months before analysis," explains Frank Tittel, an applied physicist at Rice University.

A more promising technique for early detection focuses on changes in carbon isotopes in carbon dioxide. The ratio between carbon 12 and carbon 13 is roughly 90 to one in the atmosphere, but it can differ appreciably in volcanic gases. A ratio change by as little as 0.1 part per million could signal an influx of carbon dioxide from magma either building under or rising up through the volcano.

Lasers can help detect this change: carbon 12 and 13 absorb light at slightly different mid-infrared wavelengths. The lasers must continuously tune across these wavelengths. Previously investigators used lead-salt lasers, which require liquid-nitrogen cooling and thus are impractical in the field. Furthermore, they are low-power devices, generating less than millionths of a watt, and can emit frequencies in an unstable manner. Other isotope scanning techniques are similarly lab-bound.

Tittel and other scientists in the U.S. and Britain, in partnership with the Italian government, have devised a volcano-monitoring system around a quantum-cascade laser. Such a semiconductor laser can produce high power across a wide frequency. Moreover, they are rugged and do not require liquid-nitrogen cooling, making them compact enough to fit inside a shoe box.

The researchers first tried out their device on gas emissions from Nicaraguan craters in 2000. The new field tests will check its performance and accuracy in

A Waterfall of Electrons

Quantum-cascade lasers consist of thin, nanoscale layers of semiconducting materials that provide several energy levels to an electron. An excited electron cascades down the levels to lose energy, emitting a laser photon at each step. In this way, a single electron can emit dozens of photons, making quantum-cascade lasers more powerful than standard semiconductor lasers, in which only one photon per excited electron is emitted. Moreover, by adjusting the size of the layers during fabrication, researchers can make an electron emit photons of different frequencies. The combination of high-power, wide-frequency bandwidth and compact size makes the quantum-cascade laser ideal for volcano monitoring.

harsh volcanic locales. Dirk Richter, a research engineer at the National Center for Atmospheric Research in Boulder, Colo., says it would prove difficult to design a system "to work in one of the worst and most challenging environments possible on earth," but "if there's one group in the world that dares to do this, that's Frank Tittel's group."

If the instrument works, the plan is to deploy early-warning systems of lasers around volcanoes, with each device transmitting data in real time. False alarms should not occur, because carbon isotope ratios in magma differ significantly from those in the crust. The changes that the laser helps to detect also take place over weeks to months, providing time to compare data from other instruments, as well as ample evacuation notice. "Our system aims at avoiding a catastrophe like the Vesuvius eruption," says team member Damien Weidmann, a physicist at the Rutherford Appleton Laboratory in Oxfordshire, England. Field tests for the prototype are planned for the spring of 2005 in the volcanic Alban Hills region southeast of Rome, near the summer home of Pope John Paul II, as well as for volcanic areas near Los Alamos, N.M.

Charles Choi is a freelance writer based in New York City.

Volcanic magma and fire are predictable in some respects because they operate within known scientific principles. However, many things about them remain a mystery. Like earthquakes, it is difficult for scientists to predict when and where they will occur, and what exactly will happen once they flare up. Researchers try to chart their behavior to predict what may happen in the future, but they have not yet resolved many pressing questions. In fact, author Douglas Gantenbein writes, "Fire has become the defining character-istic of the [American] West." Each decade, governments spend billions of dollars fighting fires and paying for the damage they cause. Of particular concern are crown fires, which quickly jump from treetop to treetop, creating their own wind and, as the saying goes, spreading like wildfire.

Gantenbein touches on the issue of human-induced climate change at the end of the following article. Many scientists believe that burning of fossil fuels by humans has dramatically changed the climate due to all of the pollution that is being released into the earth's atmosphere. Climate change may indirectly influence fires because it could lead to more extreme weather conditions with periods of heavy rains followed by long droughts. In addition to climate change, humans also directly affect the environment by cutting down trees and other plants, which changes the layout of forests. Fire is a natural phenomenon that can promote forest health, but the natural system of checks and balances might not work so well now, given all of the human-enacted changes. —JV

"Burning Questions"
by Douglas Gantenbein
Scientific American, November 2002

By late this past July, it seemed the entire West was ablaze. At that point, more than four million acres of forest and brushland had burned—twice the annual average in the past decade. The National Interagency

Fire Center in Boise, Idaho, the U.S. coordination center for wildfire, had been at its highest alert level for more than a month, a stage it didn't hit until August the previous year. The U.S. Forest Service was already predicting it would easily bust its annual $1-billion firefighting budget, and with other land-use agencies also facing big fire bills, it seemed 2002 might be the most expensive fire year ever. Worst of all, 15 people had been killed in fire-related mishaps, including five who died in horrifying airplane crashes when the wings of two aerial-retardant tankers peeled off in midair.

Fire Factors

Fire has become the defining characteristic of the West. From May until September, from New Mexico and Arizona to Washington, Idaho and Montana, plumes of smoke as high as 40,000 feet punctuate the horizon as tens of thousands of acres below them burn. This year some of those plumes have marked giant fires of 100,000 acres or more. In Colorado, for instance, the devastating Hayman fire scorched more than 100,000 acres and cost some $40 million to fight. In Arizona, the Rodeo fire joined with the Chediski fire to burn more than 300,000 acres. And in Oregon, the Biscuit fire consumed an astonishing 500,000 acres of forest, an area larger than all five boroughs of New York City, and forced nearly 17,000 to flee. The Biscuit fire ultimately cost $113 million to combat, making it the most expensive fire suppression effort in wildland fire history.

The reasons behind these appalling seasons of fire are many: forest management that attempted to control fires but instead made them worse, severe drought, even arson. Since the early 1960s fires have become consistently hotter and bigger. In 1961, for instance, the Sleeping Child fire in Montana burned about 28,000 acres and amazed firefighters with its ferocity. Now such a fire hardly merits special notice.

The big fire season of 2000, which saw more than eight million acres burn, prodded the federal government to do more than merely write checks in October to cover the previous summer's firefighting bill. The Clinton administration committed $1.8 billion a year to a project called the National Fire Plan. While pouring millions more into firefighting equipment and hiring new firefighters, the plan also earmarked substantial sums for fire research, which will greatly help the efforts of fire scientists.

Kevin C. Ryan is a specialist on the effects of fire on a forest—how it hurts forests, how it enhances them—at the forest service's Fire Sciences Laboratory in Missoula, Mont. In particular, he focuses on methods for determining whether a fire-damaged tree has a chance of survival, something that cannot be resolved simply by looking at whether its needles are charred. "Until now, most attention to fires has been hero worship," Ryan says, referring to the tendency to rush TV crews and reporters to the scene. "But now there's a real interest in trying to understand the scientific underpinnings of what's going on." Scientists are learning how big fires burn, how to better comprehend their impact, perhaps even how to predict what a fire will do before it does it.

One area of interest is the way in which these conflagrations burn and grow. The fires that raged in Oregon, Colorado, Arizona and other states in 2002 all were crown fires, the most devastating type. In these blazes the flames literally leap from treetop to treetop. They are impossible to fight. Not only can crown fires easily cross a five-foot firebreak scratched out by crews using Pulaskis, the combination ax/pick that after nearly 70 years remains the staple tool of firefighters, they have been known to hurdle rivers hundreds of feet wide.

Fires of this kind were once rare; during the 1910s and 1920s, firefighters deployed by the nascent forest service often could walk right up to a fire and beat it out with a blanket. Today fires commonly shoot flames 400 feet into the air, can generate temperatures of 2,000 degrees Fahrenheit and devour perhaps 35 tons of fuel an acre in just an hour. The winds they create may reach 100 miles an hour. Worse, these fires can utterly destroy forests of Ponderosa pine, the dominant tree species in the West. A big, beautiful tree that creates majestic, open forests that offer shade and sun in equal measure and provide habitat for dozens of birds, mammals and insects, the Ponderosa is supremely adapted to coexist with fire. But only frequent, small fires, not infrequent, huge ones.

"When a crown fire happens, this [Ponderosa pine] forest can't go home again," Ryan says. "What comes in next won't be a natural regime; it'll be dominated by exotic weeds and trees that couldn't exist when fire used to come through frequently." In Arizona, for instance, a 1977 crown fire near Mount Elden burned so hot that the thin volcanic soil was sterilized, and even now few Ponderosa pines, which once blanketed the site, have reemerged.

But the conditions that create such devastating fires also make them hazardous to study. "You're in harm's way if you try to plant something in front of a fire," says Don J. Latham, a fire-behavior scientist at the Fire Sciences Laboratory. "So almost all the data gathering has to be done remotely, either with aircraft or satellites." And those tools, Latham points out, can be fairly crude—good at determining the location of a fire but poor at gathering the details of what takes place inside it. Scientists are refining this information in a variety of ways.

Since the early 1960s, for example, much has been learned about the behavior of forest fires in the burn chamber of the Missoula lab. The 88-foot-tall chamber structure consists of a large central burn room and two smaller wind tunnels. During the 1960s and 1970s, fire researcher Richard Rothermel developed accurate computer models for explaining how fires spread as wind and topography change. That work came to prominence in Norman Maclean's 1992 book *Young Men and Fire*, an exploration of the 1949 Mann Gulch tragedy, in which 13 firefighters were overrun by a Montana blaze. For years, observers had wondered how young, fit smoke jumpers could be overtaken. Rothermel, who before joining the fire lab had worked on nuclear propulsion for aircraft, showed that the firefighters could not possibly have outrun a fire that moved uphill at close to seven miles per hour, faster than the tiring men could travel over the steep, rough terrain.

The Missoula burn chambers remain in regular use for, among other things, testing batches of fire retardant. Studies conducted in conjunction with Underwriters Laboratories have also helped refine a new class of water-based gels that thicken water and help it stick to the roof or the wall of a house threatened by an approaching fire.

But both the chamber and the computer models are limited. The burn chamber, where test samples such as pine needles or excelsior (fine, shredded wood often used as packing material) are ignited, creates fires that are too small to demonstrate the internal dynamics of a conflagration. Current computer models, meanwhile, allow a researcher to change wind conditions—but only those that would exist if no fire were burning. The models cannot, in other words, account for the hellacious winds created by the fire itself. But better models require better data, and forest fires are not willing research subjects.

The Flamethrower Test

The obvious solution: set a fire in a place where fuel loads, topography and weather would just about guarantee that one would break out anyway. In 1997 Latham and his fellow researchers had an opportunity to light their own crown fire in a remote part of Canada's Northwest Territories, near the town of Fort Providence. There, in the International Crown Fire Modeling Experiment, Canadian and U.S. researchers set up nine five-acre plots of black spruce and jack pine, tree species not too dissimilar from lodgepole pine, a tree that fuels severe fires in the U.S. Canadian fire scientists came in before the Montana crews, carefully measuring and weighing the fuels to determine exactly how much combustible material was there—"getting down on their hands and knees to put a ruler into the duff," as Latham put it. The scientists wired the sites with heat sensors, high-speed movie cameras, video cameras, infrared imagers, and smoke-sampling devices.

And then it was show time. The researchers drove around the sites with a flamethrower mounted on the back of a pickup truck. The results were unbelievable. One tract was immolated in minutes. Video images taken from inside the burns show an eerie glow as the fire grows in intensity. Then what look like gleaming grasshoppers bound across the screen, a wave of hot embers thrown off by the flaming trees. These in turn set new, small fires, from which the smoke is at first blown away, then sucked backed into, the approaching fire front. For one burn, firefighters' protective Nomex clothing and silvery fire shelters were placed in the flames' path. They were vaporized.

The "Natural" Solution

To help forestall today's catastrophic wildfires, some forest experts recommend that we return forests to yesterday's conditions. William Wallace Covington, a forest restoration expert at Northern Arizona University, suggests thinning Western forests from their current density of 200 trees per acre or more to a pre-1880 level of about 30 or 40 trees per acre—the level determined by how many old trees or pre-1880 tree stumps are counted on a given acre. With that goal accomplished, prescribed—or planned—fire or even natural fire could be reintroduced to forests without the risk of a huge blaze. To Covington, the stakes are enormous. "If we don't have this worked out by 2010 or 2015, we're not going to have any natural Ponderosa pine forests left," he says. "We'll have pines, but not 500-year-old ones. And people just won't know what a natural forest (in the West) looks like."

Solutions such as the one Covington proposes are gaining a sympathetic ear in U.S. Forest Service and government circles—in mid-July, Covington testified before a Senate Committee on the growing problem of wildfire. But his ideas are not without controversy. Environmental groups are deeply suspicious of activities they view as illegal logging dressed up as "restoration" and suggest that Covington's prescriptions are overly aggressive and even damaging to already fragile forests. Then there is the sheer cost of such an endeavor, which may reach as much as $700 per acre, with perhaps 100 million acres requiring attention.

Although it is more costly per acre to battle a blaze, historically policy leaders have found it easier to do that than to set aside large sums for preventive measures. By late summer, enthusiasm for such fuel-reduction programs was nonetheless building, culminating in a call by President George W. Bush for Congress to relax logging laws in areas prone to devastating wildfires.

It's not completely clear, however, that treating forests in the manner advised by Covington and others will work. To learn more, researchers have set up 13 test sites in fire-prone states including Arizona, Montana, and California. At these sites, various fuel-treatment regimes can be implemented—such as using mechanical thinning or controlled fire to remove underbrush—and the results will be measured for seven years or more. "This has just never been done before," says Bob Clark, a fire scientist in Boise, Idaho, who manages the nationwide Joint Fire Science Program that financed the fuel-test sites. "We'll be able to look at everything from how thinning affects arthropods to the plant community to fire."

Latham and his co-workers returned to the Northwest Territories in 1998 and 1999 and are continuing to digest the wealth of data taken from the tests, facts that will aid fire managers in better understanding the intensity inside a big fire and its potential to spread. For instance, the results will improve existing computer models such as Farsite (fire area simulator), a program created by Fire Sciences Lab computer expert Mark A. Finney that takes into account a site's topography, fuels and weather to show how a fire is apt to move across the countryside. The data will be useful to Latham and others in developing fire-specific models that demonstrate more precisely how small changes in a fire might affect its overall behavior, which can guide fire managers as they plot tactics.

The test burns in Canada will also help reduce the risk of fighting fires. Bret Butler, a mechanical engineer at the Fire Sciences Lab, is using the data to delve into the requirements for a "safety zone," where firefighters go if a fire threatens to overrun them. At present, a safety zone's parameters are subjective. Basically, firefighters search for as large an area as possible where rocky, moist or burned-over ground will hold back the fire. But Butler has found that even a slight change in the distance between a firefighter and a fire can greatly influence the chance of survival. A firefighter 1,100 feet from a tall fire front may live, whereas one only 100 feet closer might die. "It's a very nonlinear process," Butler says. "A small change in the distance can change the radiant energy transfer by four or five times."

But increasingly, it is electronic technology that is giving scientists new insight into forest fires. On a hazy day this past May, Fire Sciences Lab researcher

Colin C. Hardy and University of Montana forestry professor Lloyd P. Queen were working outside the lab, around what looked like one of the large, flat griddles popular in Korean-style restaurants. Next to it was a wading pool. Both devices—the griddle heated to about 400 degrees F and the pool cooled to about 70 degrees F—were wired to record their precise temperatures. A Cessna, outfitted with infrared sensors, circled overhead, so researchers could compare the temperature picked up from the air with the actual temperature of the pool and griddle.

Queen and Hardy would use the airborne infrared sensors over the summer to build an accurate thermal image of fires—how hot they burned and for how long—and compare that with other data about the fuels and forest conditions known to exist at the fire's site. Hardy, a fire-effects specialist, also hoped to use data gathered from the air to determine whether a given fire is hot enough to kill trees or merely scorch their needles, information that forest managers may use to decide whether to salvage damaged trees or allow them to recover.

Predicting the Flames

Remote Sensing—the use of infrared scanners or devices such as lidar (light detection and ranging) to study a fire's intensity and emissions from a distance—is fast coming into its own. Such applications are not new; for several years, infrared images have helped fire managers peer through the smoke and haze of a big fire to pinpoint its location and size. Satellite imagery has also helped determine these factors. "But," Queen notes, "those methods basically give us pictures, not real data. What we're trying to do is say more than 'Here is a fire.' We want to understand its thermal characteristics—therefore, 'This is the effect it might have.'"

That will be important in taking a step toward what fire scientists view as their current holy grail: knowing what a fire will burn before the fire burns it. Atop the fire lab sits a white dome, installed early this year. Inside, a satellite dish tracks NASA's Terra satellite, launched in December 1999 as part of a 15-year project to collect data about Earth [see "Monitoring Earth's Vital Signs," by Michael D. King and David D. Herring; SCIENTIFIC AMERICAN, April 2000].

Terra makes three orbits every day over North America. With each pass, its MODIS (moderate resolution imaging spectroradiometer) unit scans the planet's surface, gauging such features as snowfall or melt, cloud cover, and the spread of green grass each spring. With its fairly rough, 10-meter resolution, MODIS also picks up hot spots (fires) and relays that information to the dish atop the burn tower and next to an array of servers in a room on the fire lab's second floor. There, within minutes of the satellite's pass, researchers can spot a fire that has developed since the satellite was last overhead.

The MODIS findings may allow scientists to combine news that a fire exists with data about the fuels around the fire, the terrain across which it is burning and what the weather will do. With these facts, fire scientists could tell managers within hours of a blaze's start what it will do, how much damage it will cause if left to its own devices and where it might make the most sense to try to stop it. Or the scientists could determine that a fire may actually benefit an area that is in need of one yet is not so overgrown that a burn would become catastrophic. At least that is the tantalizing prospect. Whether fire managers and the politicians to whom they answer will ever feel completely comfortable allowing a computer model to make the call remains to be seen.

Uncertain as well is whether the West's fire problem can be solved with human intervention. To simply let fires burn is intolerable: the environmental havoc they cause is tremendous, endangering animals such as the Mexican spotted owl and bighorn sheep in addition to threatening the vast Ponderosa pine ecosystem. Then there is the human cost, as people's lives are disrupted and property destroyed or damaged. But no amount of dollars or firefighters can stop a big fire once it gets moving, making the summer's showy firefighting efforts increasingly fruitless. One solution offered is to turn back the clock on forests, re-creating woodlands that look like they did before European settlers brought sheep and the forest service brought firefighting hotshot crews.

In any event, fires will threaten the West for years to come, with climate change perhaps influencing them in ways not yet foreseen. But science is working hard to understand the danger fires pose and to help mitigate their impact.

The Author

Douglas Gantenbein is the Seattle correspondent for the Economist *and also contributes to* Air & Space Smithsonian, Travel and Leisure, Outside, This Old House *and other magazines. He is writing a book about forest fires in the American West.*

We all know that germs can travel in the air. If someone has the flu and sneezes in a crowded room, some people in that room might breathe in the germs and become ill. In this scenario, however, the germs do not have to travel very far. A scarier possibility is that disease-inducing viruses, bacteria, and fungi can attach themselves to dust, which is known to travel considerable distances.

Author Otto Pohl begins his article with a description of a Sahara dust storm. Unbelievably, the dust blew out of Africa and up to the United Kingdom, where it may have led to an outbreak of foot-and-mouth disease, which mostly affects livestock. Newly emerging human diseases such as SARS may spread in such a way, although medical experts are not

*yet certain of this. To examine the possibility,
NASA researchers and other scientists are
monitoring dust activity on a global scale. They
hope to learn more about how dust storms
may affect the health of animals, including
humans, both on land and in the oceans.*

*As if nature is not scary enough at times,
humans now present another threat involving
dust germs. Terrorists may be able to store
germs in dust, which they can distribute over
large areas. A terrorist potentially could sicken
an entire city using the deadly dust, so scientists
continue to consider this possibility.* —JV

"Disease Dustup"
by Otto Pohl
Scientific American, July 2003

On February 11, 2001, an enormous cloud of dust
whipped out of the Sahara Desert and moved north
across the Atlantic, reaching the U.K. two days later. A
few days afterward, counties across the island began
reporting simultaneous outbreaks of foot-and-mouth
disease, a viral sickness of livestock (sometimes confused
with mad cow disease). For Eugene Shinn, a geologist
at the U.S. Geological Survey in St. Petersburg, Fla.,
that coincidence suggested an obvious link.

The idea that large-scale disease outbreaks could be
caused by dust clouds from other continents has been
floating around for years. But it seemed far-fetched. In

the U.S. government, "no one wanted to listen to me," Shinn remembers about his proposal that something as amorphous and uncontrollable as a dust cloud could bring the disease to America.

But the theory is now gaining acceptance as scientists find that it may explain many previously mysterious disease outbreaks. Although the world's dry areas have always shed dust into the atmosphere— wind blows more than a billion tons of dust around the planet every year—the globe's dust girdle has become larger in recent years. Some of the changes are part of nature's cycles, such as the 30-year drought in northern Africa. Others, including the draining of the Aral Sea in Central Asia and the overdependence on Lake Chad in Africa, are the result of shortsighted resource management. Poor farming practices also hasten desertification, creating dust beds polluted with pesticides and laced with diseases from human and animal waste.

For Shinn and his co-workers, it was a strange disease outbreak in the Caribbean in the early 1980s that first brought to mind the connection between dust and disease. A soil fungus began to attack and kill seafan coral. The researchers doubted that local human activity was the culprit, because the disease was found even in uninhabited places and islands devoid of soil. In addition, Garriet W. Smith of the University of South Carolina demonstrated that because the soil fungus could not multiply in seawater, it required a constant fresh supply to continue spreading.

Leaving DDT in the Dust

Dust carries more than just disease. Ginger Garrison of the U.S. Geological Survey suspects that DDE, a breakdown product of DDT and a dangerous endocrine disruptor, is blowing over from Africa to the Caribbean. She is currently analyzing dust samples from Mali, the Caribbean and the ocean areas in between. She has also visited Mali to track the source of these toxic dust-borne chemicals. "There has been a definite change in what goes into the air in West Africa," she says. "In the past 12 to 15 years, there has been an incredible increase in the use of pesticides and plastics incineration."

Smith analyzed the African dust blowing across the Caribbean and was able to isolate and cultivate the soil fungus *Aspergillus sydowii*, with which he infected healthy seafans. USGS investigators then showed how the *Aspergillus* fungus and other organisms could survive the long trip from Africa protected by dense clouds of dust.

Researchers are now finding evidence that supports the link between sickness and dust. Ginger Garrison of the USGS believes that there is a direct link between bacteria-caused coral diseases such as white plague and black-band disease and African dust storm activity. In addition, outbreaks of foot-and-mouth disease in South Korea last year followed large dust storms blowing in from Mongolia and China.

Other organizations are now joining the USGS in tracking dust. NASA has satellites that are carefully monitoring dust storms, which can cover an area as large as Spain. The National Oceanic and Atmospheric Administration has just opened a station in California to track Asian dust as it passes over the U.S. (Although the SARS virus could theoretically cross oceans in a dust storm, the epidemiology so far indicates that person-to-person contact is the only way SARS has spread.)

The findings on international dust storms have also attracted the attention of those who are concerned about bioterrorism. "Anthrax will certainly make the trip" in dust from Africa to the U.S., remarks Shinn, who recently completed a terrorism risk assessment for the U.S. Dust clouds could be considered, in effect, a very dirty bomb.

Otto Pohl is based in Berlin.

In the Western world, most of us tend not to associate lakes with natural disasters, except, perhaps, for flooding. In fact, many people build vacation homes near lakes and travel to lake sites for picnics and other leisure activities. The next article, then, might come as a shock if you have not yet heard about lakes that can kill with little or no warning.

Author Marguerite Holloway discusses a particular lake in Cameroon, Africa, that killed one man's entire family and at least 1,700 other people. The way in which the lake killed the people was particularly insidious. Carbon dioxide gas and other materials dissolve in water that remains separate from the freshwater seen at the top of the lake. The activated water remains at the bottom of the lake until wind or some other trigger releases the pressure and the deadly gas.

This article addresses an important dilemma faced by many leaders and scientists today. Geologists probably can monitor such lakes and use equipment to slowly release the pent-up gas, but this kind of effort would require substantial money and manpower. —JV

"The Killing Lakes"
by Marguerite Holloway
Scientific American, July 2000

Mohammed Musa Abdulahi woke one Saturday morning to find he couldn't feel or move his right arm. He remembered he hadn't been feeling well, that he had gone to lie down inside the schoolhouse instead of taking care of the younger students, as he sometimes did. He got up, his arm hanging uselessly at his side, and prodded his friend, who also had come inside to take a nap. The friend jolted awake, cried out for no apparent reason and raced away. Abdulahi started to walk home through his village in northwestern Cameroon and found it horrifyingly silent. The dirt roads and yards of Subum were littered with corpses. People lay unmoving on the ground, as if they had fallen suddenly while in the middle of a stroll or a conversation. The dogs were dead. The cattle were dead. Birds and insects had dropped from the trees.

Abdulahi made his way to his father's house, only to find that his entire family was also dead—his brothers and sisters, his father and his father's two wives. For a moment, though, there was a small hope. He touched one of the babies, and it began to cry. Abdulahi tried to pick it up, but couldn't because of his lifeless arm, so he made a crude sling out of cloth. When he touched the baby again, it too was dead.

"It is terrible to be without a family," he says. "Everything you do, you feel not quite right." Abdulahi tells me his story as we sit on the southern shore of Lake Nyos, the very lake that spewed a cloud of lethal gas on the evening of Thursday, August 21, 1986, killing all 11 members of his family and at least 1,700 other people. The very lake that could explode again at any moment. It is the first time Abdulahi has returned since the disaster—since he spent two days in the coma that somehow saved him—and he is now a tall young man of 29. "It is not that I made a decision not to come back," he says in his calm way. "It is just fate now."

It is indeed strange circumstance that has united Abdulahi and an international team of scientists who have come to Cameroon to study the deadly lake in order to disarm it, if they ultimately can. Earlier this afternoon Abdulahi walked down the mountains from the town of Eseh to the lake in his tan overcoat, black pants and black-and-white checked shirt. He brought a dapper presence to the shore's chaos of monitoring equipment, raft-building supplies, inflatable boats, tents, coolers, mangy dogs, soon-to-be-cooked chickens,

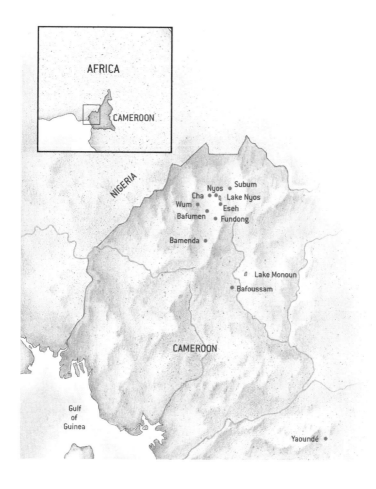

and frenzied, unwashed scientists—and one unkempt journalist—surrounded by their entourage of several dozen local visitors. A day or so earlier a driver on his way to meet the team at Lake Nyos had asked for directions in the city of Bamenda and had procured Abdulahi as a guide. Only a week after he had watched a broadcast about the team's arrival in Yaoundé, the capital, and had wondered how he could become involved, Mohammed Musa Abdulahi found himself camping next to Lake Nyos, taking part in the project.

For the team members, their October 1999 arrival in Yaoundé had also marked a beginning. Since 1986 scientists studying Lake Nyos have sought to rid the lake of the deadly gas that accumulates in its bottom waters before it explodes again and kills thousands more. Degassing the lake is technologically straightforward—and in the context of natural-disaster prevention, easy and cheap. Yet accomplishing this relatively simple task has proved astonishingly difficult. Despite the clear urgency of the problem and the unique opportunity to forestall natural disaster, little has been done to protect the people around Lake Nyos. Politics, lack of financial support (because of the reactive rather than preventive orientation of some funding organizations), and miscommunication have all inter-fered. But in Yaoundé—despite the persistent and worrisome flickering of some of these same problems—it appeared things were finally about to happen.

Nyos is a stunning lake, surrounded variously by cultivated fields, cathedral-like rock faces and verdant hills. On the afternoon of Abdulahi's arrival it looks gray and glass-flat calm. But in its depths, Nyos is active. It is a crater lake, one formed by a volcanic eruption about five centuries ago that left a plug of magma at the bottom of the crater. This plug cooled and the depression filled with water, 210 meters deep. It is one of many such lakes found the world over in volcanic chains—but one of only two, it appears, that have ever exploded and taken human life. The other one, Lake Monoun, lies just 95 kilometers to the southeast.

From deep volcanic activity, carbon dioxide (CO_2) gas rises up until it meets groundwater beneath the lake, dissolves into that water and flows into Nyos, carrying with it minerals, themselves dissolved by the reactive gas. It accumulates in solution, staying separate from the upper layers of freshwater. In most crater lakes the lower water periodically turns over, bringing any gas-rich water to the surface, where the gas diffuses harmlessly into the atmosphere. But Nyos and Monoun do not turn over. The boundary, called the chemocline, between the mineralized, dense deep water and the fresh upper water stays dangerously intact. (Similar conditions prevail at Lake Kivu in Rwanda and the Democratic Republic of Congo, although there is no record of its having ever erupted.)

In these lakes the gas saturates the bottom water until some trigger—a strong wind, a violent storm, cool weather that causes a pocket of upper water to sink, a landslide, an earthquake, no one knows—provokes a bit of deep water to move upward. No longer strong-armed by pressure, the carbon dioxide comes out of solution; it bubbles to the surface, pulling more bottom water with it. It is thought that this uprising gains momentum, a few bubbles becoming a stream of bubbles and then, like champagne finally uncorked, the gas-laden water erupts in a great fountain—at Nyos, the jet was 80 meters high—and carbon dioxide fills the air.

A weighty gas, half again as heavy as air, carbon dioxide hugs the ground, suffocating anything in its path. When Lake Monoun exploded on August 15, 1984, 37 people were killed. Lake Nyos, which is larger and deeper, was more devastating. The cloud of gas rolled down the hills at an estimated 72 kilometers per hour, into valleys and villages up to 20 kilometers away. According to George W. Kling—a University of Michigan biologist who has extensively studied both lakes and who is the leader of the team Abdulahi has joined—the last person to die was a girl who, the morning after the explosion, descended into a ravine where the gas hung, heavy and low. Abdulahi thinks he and his friend were saved because they were sleeping in a room that somehow, despite the open door, protected them from the full onslaught of gas. Abdulahi slept for about two days, and because of lying on his right arm for so long was unable to use it for several months. Abdulahi believes the gas disturbed his friend's mind— an observation that is consistent with reports of disorientation in many of the survivors.

Lake Nyos is clearly poised to kill again, as is Lake Monoun. According to the most recent calculations by

Kling and chemist William C. Evans of the U.S. Geological Survey, Lake Nyos contains twice as much carbon dioxide as was released during the explosion (0.4 cubic kilometer today, as opposed to only 0.17 cubic kilometer in 1986). Another explosion could also rupture the fragile dam, or spillway, at the northern end of the lake, and the waters could flow as far as Nigeria—drowning or displacing as many as 10,000 people. Although the area around the lake was evacuated after the disaster and 3,500 or so refugees resettled in safe places, many people are again living nearby, drawn by the land's richness. Cornfields abut the water's edge on the southern side. Cattle graze the hills around the lake under the watchful eyes of their Fulani herders. And in the early 1990s some European scientist released tilapia into the fishless lake in an uncontrolled and unauthorized experiment. The fish thrived, altering the ecosystem in unknown ways and becoming another incentive luring people to the lake. With few resources or possibilities for earning a living, the impoverished people of the area have little choice but to approach the deceptively benign-looking waters of Nyos.

Perhaps fortunately, the enormous difficulty of reaching this beautiful spot keeps outsiders away. Its remoteness, however, also makes it hard to study and degas. Five days after arriving in Yaoundé, we set out for Nyos in four vehicles. Part of the team—Evans; Kling and his assistant, Karen J. Riseng; Minoru Kusakabe of Okayama University and four of his colleagues from various institutions in Japan; Gregory Tanyileke of the

Cameroonian Institute-for Geological and Mining Research (IRGM) and I—take our places in two rented Nissan Patrols with their drivers. The others, including Tanyileke's IRGM colleagues—Hubert Mvogo, Jacob Nwalal, Paul Nia and Justin Nlozoa—drive two trucks laden with equipment. We travel to Bamenda in comfort, passing logging trucks with some of Cameroon's remaining old-growth forests stacked high on their backs, passing red cocoa beans that smell like vinegar and fluffy white manioc spread on the side of the highway to dry. We spend the night in a hotel, pick up supplies—including 36 rolls of pink toilet paper for 14 people—and head to the end of the paved road at Fundong. (We later run out of fresh water. We still have toilet paper.)

The single road heading north from Fundong is ghastly and effectively isolates the region around Lake Nyos. It is more a series of vast muddy pits, connected, on a dry day, by an uneven dusty trail, than it is a road. For 13 kilometers we slip and slide and lurch and stick, and the sway bar on one of the Nissans breaks. By late afternoon it is clear that despite Kling's frustration we can't get any farther than the village of Bafumen. Members of the Japanese team wisely find a house to stay in, and the rest of us pitch our tents in a cemetery, right below a memorial to victims of the Nyos disaster. Lake Nyos is just 17 or so kilometers away now, but it seems as inaccessible as Yaoundé. And word about town is that the bridge on the road to Eseh has been washed out.

We start out the next morning with fresh faith. The sway bar had been soldered back together, and the evening's chill softened by Bafumen's supply of warm beer. After repairing the first flat of the day, we reach the bridge. It hasn't been washed out. The left side is, in fact, intact. Only the right side is falling into the river. The entire team descends from the vehicles, and there is much scientific and highly technical muttering about mass and stability and speed and load and distribution, in the midst of which Mvogo jumps in the equipment truck he commands—"The Grandmother"—and speeds her across. By the end of the day we have reached Eseh, spent hours waiting out a downpour, and have set up camp after hiring the entire town to carry, on their heads, all our things—including the hard, heavy suitcases infelicitously packed by team members who thought we would be driving right to the water's edge—the six kilometers down the steep slippery-when-wet path to the lake. In the middle of camp we place a blue crate filled with canisters of oxygen: 10 minutes apiece for just 10 of us. (Some of us initially try to set up our tents on a hill so that we will be safer if the lake decides to explode again. But it proves too difficult, and with a small but nagging fear we pitch below in the main camp.)

The first task the next morning is raft building. After the explosion in 1986 Kling and his colleagues set up a climate station on a raft in the middle of the lake to monitor temperature, wind, sun and rainfall. That station, beaten ragged by the weather, no longer functions, and the raft needs replacing. In addition, the team needs to install thermistors that will hang from the new raft at nine different depths to record changes in temperature—which reflect the movements and chemistry of the lake's waters. They also need to lower probes to measure the carbon dioxide's pressure. Only once these instruments are in place will it be safe to think about a major degassing. Every stage of that operation must be observed to see if it is dangerously altering conditions. So the first order of business is to build a raft sturdy enough to hold the new climate station, to anchor the various probes, and, if possible, to provide a large enough platform from which the scientists can drop canisters to collect water so they can measure carbon dioxide concentrations. The Japanese contingent, under the direction of engineer Yutaka Yoshida of Yoshida Consulting Engineer Office in Iwate, Japan, takes charge of building the raft.

By the time Abdulahi arrives in camp two days later, the raft has been completed and the climate station assembled and attached to it. Abdulahi finds room in one of the tents and borrows some clothes for his stay. The following day he helps Evans and Riseng with their work. The thermistors need to be unwound, marked for depth and taped firmly together for stability, so Riseng sends her assistants to the far ends of the cornfields with the long wires that will stretch nearly to the lake bottom. Seventeen men are scattered between the bright-green plants, wires draped over their shoulders—one of them, 201 meters away, is barely visible on the horizon of a field. Abdulahi helps Riseng rewind the thermistors and then decides to brave a trip on the lake, where he checks the anchors for the new raft with Evans and Tanyileke. The sun is blindingly hot. Some of us sit around camp in a stupor. A Fulani gentleman brings a gift of avocados. The day stretches on.

Abdulahi comes back from the lake. He now has one of the walkie-talkies and has become a field coordinator, helping everyone find what, or whom, they need. We sit on a box of equipment and—between static-pocked demands from the transmitter—talk about his desire for a family. He says he has met a woman he wants to marry and who wants to marry him, but her family has objected. They are hoping for a rich suitor instead of an electrical engineer, the occupation Abdulahi chose years ago. "Why is this happening?" he asks sadly. "First my family, now a wife."

With the raft done, the instruments down and water samples collected, Kling and his colleagues have set the stage for the degassing operation that will, with luck, commence this fall or winter. Over the past several years, Kusakabe and Yoshida prepared a $3-million plan to degas the lakes that was submitted to the Japanese International Cooperation Agency by the Cameroonian government. Their design entails running 12 pipes into Nyos, at three different depths, and allowing the CO_2-laden water to froth up, perhaps at the initial rate of 320 kilometers per hour, to release its gas. They envision three such pipes at Monoun.

This idea has been around, in various iterations, since Lake Nyos exploded. And a version has been tested on both lakes. In 1992 Michel Halbwachs of the University of Savoy secured funding from the French government and the European Community to do a preliminary degassing test in Monoun. Halbwachs and his colleagues, Tanyileke among them, lowered a five- and a 14-centimeter-diameter pipe and, using a motorized pump, sucked up some bottom water. Because of the pressure differential, a self-sustaining fountain of gas rich water gushed up in both pipes, and carbon dioxide diffused away. They were able to close valves in the pipes to shut off the release.

The success of the Monoun project led to a similar effort in 1995 at Lake Nyos. With money from Gaz de France, Halbwachs and others lowered a 14-centimeter-wide, 205-meter-long pipe. Things did not go as smoothly as they had at Monoun, however, and after the fountain started, the pipe rose, terrifyingly, from the bottom. Fortunately, no explosion was triggered, and the experiments suggested degassing was feasible.

Halbwachs had a different plan from Yoshida and Kusakabe's. His entailed only five pipes for Nyos and a remote on-off switch that could be controlled via satellite from France. Although the scientists met in Yaoundé in October to hash out their disagreements, and appeared to do so, the conflict emerged a day later at a public meeting with members of a newly formed Cameroonian interministerial committee on degassing. Halbwachs presented his five-pipe plan, and Kusakabe presented the 12-pipe version. The ministers focused on the discord, and for a short and wrenching time it looked as though the entire project was going to be derailed.

Ultimately, Henri Hogbe Nlend, minister of scientific research and technology and head of the committee, reassured everyone that the disagreements were petty. "Any number they give now is false, everything is an estimate," he said forcefully. "The technology that they have explained will keep evolving." No one, he added, should expect the architects of a cathedral to supply specifics in the face of such a great enterprise. Uniting the various ministries behind the operation had been a monumental task. Without their combined support, the roads would not be improved, the areas around the lakes would not be evacuated, and the Cameroonian military would not be present at the degassings with oxygen tanks in case of an explosion. Minister Nlend, apparently, was not going to let some minor grievances thwart the project. And all the scientists are collaborating again.

The disagreement was atypical for a community that has been largely collaborative for more than a decade. The debate is partly the result of scientific disagreement, but in truth, the differences in designs are negligible. It appears to have resulted more from a lack of communication among the researchers about, or during, their efforts to get funding. Halbwachs felt excluded from work for which he had laid the foundation. The others say they were pursuing funding catch-as-catch-can, thinking all along that Halbwachs would work with them. "We have always assumed that anyone who cares about these lakes is working together," Kling says.

Securing funding for the project has indeed been a desperate venture. Here are two lakes that will explode, thousands of people at risk and an easy solution that could cost as little as $1 million. And yet. Although various researchers have received support from their governments or their institutions to study the lakes, it has frustrated many of them that they have not been able to get money to degas them. In 1992, for instance, a meeting on degassing was organized with the support of UNESCO and the United Nations Development Program. But neither institution put forth money for the actual project, Kling says. The scientists have tried some other channels with little success. Kling and a colleague tried to interest oil companies—which have a powerful, lucrative presence in Cameroon. No luck. And the same year as the U.N. conference, Kling appealed to the U.S. Agency for International Development (AID) and was refused because at that time the agency was not inclined to fund projects in Cameroon. After helping the victims just after the disasters, "AID had disengaged somewhat," explains Christina Neal, a geologist in the agency's Office of Foreign Disaster Assistance (OFDA). "Cameroon had a problem with democracy and good governance."

Kusakabe's efforts to get money from the Japanese International Cooperation Agency came to naught as well. Some say the Japanese government wasn't as committed to the degassing as it was to other projects in Cameroon. Others say that the Cameroonian government, which had to rate the project as the number-one aid priority to receive funds, couldn't reach consensus and that one minister favored a well in his village instead.

The politics may never be fully plumbed, but the larger issue is that many aid organizations are responsive, not preventive. Many people within this community have emphasized the dangers of this approach. But OFDA's Neal says it has only lately begun to change and points to recent mitigation efforts at AID and the Federal Emergency Management Agency. "I think at AID there has been a learning process and a cultural shift in the past few years that mitigation is increasingly the important way to approach problems and that by running in after an earthquake or merely saving bodies and providing first aid, we don't do anything for the long-term problem," she says.

It is in great part because of Neal's interest in Cameroon and its lakes and because of her strong belief in mitigation that $433,000 finally came through for Kling and the team last fall. The OFDA grant was triggered by the eruption of Mount Cameroon in the spring of 1999. The office sent John P. Lockwood, formally of the U.S. Geological Survey, who had studied Lake Nyos, to determine the extent of the danger. After meeting with U.S. Embassy representatives in

Yaounde and Cameroonian scientists and ministers, he concluded that if OFDA really wanted to help Cameroon, it should do something about the lakes.

Although the degassing seems to be on track now, many researchers still feel somehow guilty—as though they should have done something more and because they didn't know exactly what to do. Tanyileke worries that he and the others were not clear enough about the danger—at least not in a way that moved anyone to act. "We, the scientists, are still wondering, was it enough to just send reports to everyone?" says Tanyileke one late afternoon at Nyos. We are sitting on a cooler in the sun, and the weight of the heat even late in the day is leaden, stupefying. "They weren't strong enough to make them sit up."

As we talk, a nine-person delegation from Nyos village arrives. They are arrayed in finery—hats, umbrellas, bright robes—and bring a letter from their chief, Fon Tang-Nembong: "Our dear visitor we are very very happy to see you people here in our lake. We here to say will come to you all." Tanyileke describes what the team is doing and why. "An explosion could happen any day," he warns, adding "if we are doing anything that is going against your traditions, you must tell us." All the members of the team, but Tanyileke and Evans in particular, try to explain their work to the people they meet.

Such communication is crucial for many reasons, not just for good relations. It encourages people to be wary of the seemingly safe lake. It fosters scientific awareness that Tanyileke hopes will contribute to making Nyos a research center once the lake is degassed. And, finally, it helps to quell an unhelpful rumor. The rumor began, according to anthropologist Eugenia Shanklin of the College of New Jersey, when a priest who visited the devastated villages described the scene as resembling the aftermath of a neutron bomb. And so the bomb story was born. One version has Americans and Israelis detonating the device to get to diamonds under the lake. Another has a blond-haired Peace Corps worker placing the bomb so that Americans could live in the region.

The rumor rankles the team—and the Peace Corps and the U.S. Embassy in Yaoundé and, perhaps, the Israeli medics who provided disaster relief in 1986—and could interfere with evacuation efforts during the degassing if some of those same groups participate. But Shanklin finds the emergence of a modern myth intriguing—just as intriguing as the region's ancient tales. One of the legends suggests that what happened at Nyos and Monoun is not without precedent: a myth of the Kom people describes a lake that suddenly exploded and decimated a tribe.

For their part, the delegation from Nyos doesn't seem suspicious of the team's work. "We are very happy for your coming here," Tamaki Chethe says. "Everyone in Nyos is sick from this gas." And then, in a request as remarkable as Abdulahi's foray on the lake, a member of the delegation asks to taste the water that killed many of his relatives. With Abdulahi standing nearby, Tanyileke offers him some of the carbonated water collected right near the bottom. Everyone gathers around, and, in turn, they drink from the depths of their lake.

3 | Storms

Hurricanes are violent storms that usually involve lightning and rain but always have strong winds. For a storm to be classified a hurricane, the winds must exceed seventy-four miles per hour. Consequently, all hurricanes are potentially dangerous. People in the path of a hurricane should evacuate the area, but some researchers who know a lot about weather dynamics follow hurricanes and even fly into them. In the next article, journalist Tim Beardsley accompanies a scientific team on a flight into 1999's Hurricane Dennis, which mostly affected parts of Florida and surrounding states.

All hurricanes have an eye. This is a calm central area surrounded by dark clouds. The clouds make up the eyewall, where pressure changes generate most of the hurricane's winds. If researchers in a sturdy craft situate themselves in the eye or around it, they can follow the storm and conduct experiments with less risk of injury. The goal of Beardsley's flight was to determine whether the ocean below or the winds above exert more force on storms. Since this flight took place several years ago, scientists have had a *chance to analyze the data. It now appears that water droplets from the ocean can turn storms into hurricanes. Wind suspends the water in the air and the change in pressure strengthens winds. —JV*

"Dissecting a Hurricane"
by **Tim Beardsley**
Scientific American, **March 2000**

MacDill Air Force Base, Florida, August 29, 1999, 1:52 PM: Safety lectures are over and everyone is strapped into our four-engine WP3D turboprop plane, known affectionately as *Miss Piggy*. The aircraft, jammed with computers, four different radars and a variety of other instruments, is at last surging down the runway. The past few hours have been a metaphorical whirlwind: quickly arranged travel, a 6 AM flight from Baltimore, then briefing sessions with the flight crew interspersed with hurried explanations from Frank D. Marks, the lead scientist on the flight.

Our destination is a real whirlwind: Hurricane Dennis, now swirling 290 kilometers east of Jacksonville, Fla., powering 145-kilometer-per-hour winds and menacing the Carolinas. On land fearful vacationers and residents on North Carolina's barrier islands are boarding up windows, throwing bags into cars and fleeing the coming storm. But Marks and his fellow scientists from the National Oceanic and Atmospheric Administration regard Dennis with hope rather than dread. If our flight through its curved arms goes as planned, this storm will shed light on a central mystery about hurricanes and typhoons: whether it is the ocean below or the winds above that wield more power in determining whether a storm will swell to greater fury or unwind into a harmless region of low pressure.

Marks is among those pushing the idea that the ocean controls how hurricanes evolve by either adding or removing energy in the form of heat. Today's forecasting models, in contrast, treat the ocean as a passive bystander.

These models have conspicuously failed to predict when storms will intensify. Hurricane Andrew startled forecasters in 1992 when it intensified abruptly while passing over the warm waters of the Gulf Stream; it later killed 15 people and destroyed property worth $25 billion in southern Florida. In 1995 in the Gulf of Mexico, Hurricane Opal transformed overnight— after the 11 PM television news assured Gulf Coast residents that they had little to fear—from a Category 2 to a Category 4 terror capable of extreme devastation. Opal, too, had just passed over an eddy of deep warm water. Although the storm ebbed somewhat before coming ashore, it caused more than 28 deaths altogether. And earlier in 1999 Hurricane Bret followed what now seemed to be an emerging pattern, escalating from Category 2 to 4 after passing over warm water. Fortunately, it made landfall over unpopulated farmland in Texas.

If Marks and his colleagues are right, by analyzing in detail the heart of a hurricane they should be able to tease apart the web of factors that drive the storms to live, grow and die. The scientists will need to learn the temperature of the sea at different depths during the hurricane's passage. They will also want to know as much as possible about its winds and waves.

Dennis, now a strong Category 2 hurricane, has the same ominous potential for rapid intensification as Andrew and Opal did. When Hurricane Bonnie crossed the Gulf Stream in 1998—without intensifying—Marks had been frustrated by a lack of instruments to study it. But as he watched Dennis's course in late August, he recognized an opportunity. Equipment was available, and by good fortune Eric D'Asaro of the University of Washington had just dropped three high-tech floats in an east-west line across Dennis's path. The floats move up and down, monitoring temperature and salinity in the so-called mixed layer between the sea surface and about 200 meters' depth. These data could complement observations made from *Miss Piggy*. Marks scrambled his air team to launch a detailed examination of Dennis, which is what brought us to the jetway.

Our group will scan the storm from the inside out, penetrate it with falling probes, take its temperature and clock its winds. Over the past few days NOAA's Gulfstream IV jet has charted atmospheric conditions at various altitudes in the region. Our flight is to be the crux of the assessment: four straight passes through the eye of the tempest.

Marks has weathered dozens of routine flights through hurricanes, and he likes to quip that the most dangerous part of a sortie is the drive to the airport. But he also knows that the pilots face real challenges, especially near the deep banks of cumulonimbus clouds that mark the eye wall. Winds there change speed and direction unpredictably, and intense tornado-like vortices can appear with no warning. Ten years ago Marks was flying in our sister plane, *Kermit*, through Hurricane Hugo as the storm escalated to a Category 5. An engine failed while the plane was at low altitude inside the eye, and a vortex almost threw the plane into the sea. "I am lucky to be alive after that," Marks recounts.

This morning the crew displayed an easy bravado during the preflight briefing. Some experienced members sport badges on their blue flight suits celebrating the number of eye penetrations they have survived. But as we move up Florida's eastern coast, the flight engineer seems to enjoy reminding me that hurricanes can change their character within a few hours. Our flight could last nine or more. It seems important to count the number of people on board: 19, including six scientists as well as observers, instrument technicians and the flight crew.

The frailty of the complex equipment we are carrying is suddenly underscored when technician James Barr announces that the Doppler radar in the plane's tail is not producing intelligible data. This device, along with a second radar in the belly of the fuselage, can reveal wind speeds wherever rain is falling. Marks says we definitely want this information. The flight director approves a hold, and we fly in a circle while Barr and lead electronics technician Terry Lynch attempt a repair. They yank out equipment racks and swap a transmitter.

Ten minutes pass, but something is not right. Lynch is muttering under his breath and looking worried. After a few more anxious minutes, he declares victory. Everyone gets back to work.

At our starting point for the mission proper, off the coast a few kilometers north of the Florida-Georgia border, electrical engineer Richard McNamara takes the metallized plastic wrapping off a Global Positioning System (GPS) dropwindsonde. This device, which will be dropped into the storm, unfurls a parachute when it is in free fall and radios back its position to the plane. McNamara programs it by plugging it into his instrument rack for a few seconds, detaches it and places it in a transparent launch tube set in the floor. The flight director gives the "3, 2, 1," and then McNamara presses a trigger. The cabin air pressure blows the meter-long cylinder out of the fuselage with a loud whistling sound, and McNamara confirms the time.

Within seconds his workstation has acquired a signal: the sonde's parachute has deployed. He tracks the probe's location as Dennis whips it away from the plane, betraying the direction and the strength of the winds during its descent to the ocean. He will repeat this routine numerous times during the mission, gradually building a three-dimensional picture of the storm.

We are now heading east at 4,300 meters. The cheery banter of the early part of the flight has dwindled, and I feel a mounting excitement. As the coast recedes behind us and dark gray clouds loom ahead, the crew tap away at keyboards controlling a suite of instruments that will make Dennis the most minutely analyzed storm ever.

At 3:15 PM our imperturbable pilot, Ron Phillipsborn, comes on the intercom to warn of "weather" ahead. Dense rain now streams over the windows, and the blue sky we set off in is nowhere to be seen: only whiteness all about. People have been walking in the plane since we reached our cruising altitude, but now everyone heads to their seats to strap in.

The ride remains fairly smooth, however, and soon foot traffic in the aisle resumes. The spiral form winding on the radar screens is familiar from the Weather Channel, but it is far more compelling at this moment. Operators compile the maps every 30 minutes and send them by a slow satellite link to the National Hurricane Center at Florida International University in Miami. Researcher Christopher W. Landsea, furiously editing data at one of the consoles, estimates Dennis's eye to be 80 kilometers in diameter, which is larger than that of most hurricanes. The storm is moving slowly northward, brushing the coast. Its waves are now pounding jetties as its winds tear the shingles off roofs.

When we reach the point where we have to fire a probe called an Airborne Expendable Bathythermograph, or AXBT, McNamara flips a switch on his console. An explosive charge shoots the first of the AXBTs, which are preloaded in the plane's belly, out into the storm now engulfing us. AXBTs do nothing as they fall, but when they splash into the ocean they send a thermometer on a wire down to 300 meters and radio the temperature readings along the way.

We approach the eye wall at about 500 kph, shooting out more GPS sondes and AXBTs as we go. Through occasional gaps in the dense clouds I can see the roiling ocean surface, flecked generously with patches of white.

These regions of bubbles, caused when the wind blows the tops off waves, look insubstantial in comparison to the cubic kilometers of air and water heaving all around us. But scientists suspect that they are crucial in determining how a hurricane will change, because they efficiently transfer energy between sea and air. One of the instruments we are carrying, a radiometer, can measure that foaminess by detecting microwave energy reflecting off the sea surface at six different frequencies. It can in principle, anyway. In practice, software glitches have so far hung up the device on all of its previous flights. Marks is hoping that NOAA scientist Peter Black, who is grounded in Florida with a cold, succeeded in his latest attempt to debug the code.

The fuselage shudders and heaves again, and my coffee makes a bid to escape from its plastic cup.

Phillipsborn orders us back to our seats once more, but the floor and the seatbacks are now moving targets. We endure a couple of stomach-churning lurches. I start to wonder exactly how much the wings could flap like that before breaking off. McNamara, sitting across the aisle from me, is unfazed, repeatedly firing off GPS sondes alternated with an occasional AXBT. He seems too busy for any idle speculation.

I realize that the nausea-inducing plunges have stopped: we have pierced Dennis's eye. Overhead is the blue sky we left behind. Wind speed outside is about three knots, hardly enough to lift a flag. We hunt for the point where wind speed and pressure are lowest, to get a fix on the center. Not many kilometers distant, huge stacks of rain clouds are visible, strewn in a vast arc. We plunge into the eastern eye wall, dropping more sondes as we do so into the colossal heat engine turning around our plane.

Hours pass as we trace a compass rose centered on the eye. My tension has prevented hunger, but in the late afternoon I cautiously maneuver toward the galley for a sandwich, where I find a crew member calmly reading a newspaper.

The unpredictable drops become familiar but worsen on a slow upwind leg. The repaired Doppler radar is working imperfectly: its output will be less complete than Marks had wanted. Landsea announces that the instrument shows surface winds have reached about 160 kph. Dennis is indeed getting stronger. Yet as it intensifies, it stirs up cooler water from the depths. I learn later that Dennis cooled the water off the Georgia and South Carolina coasts by three degrees Celsius and roughly doubled the depth of the mixed water layer beneath its core. That effect in turn cooled Hurricane Floyd's fury when it passed the same way days later.

We are transmitting readings from the radiometer to the National Hurricane Center. But Marks is still uneasy about the device. Partway through the flight, he is surprised when the plane's radio operator patches through a phone call from Black. It must be urgent, because the radio interferes with the radars, so Marks figures he will be hearing about some new radiometer problem. In fact, Black exclaims that the instrument, which can reveal surface winds in detail, is working perfectly. Marks is sufficiently relieved to announce the good news over the intercom. The mood on the plane brightens noticeably.

The flight wears on. We make a long traverse over D'Asaro's floats, dropping AXBTs and GPS sondes as the whiteness outside fades into the black of night. On the fourth pass through the eye we again hunt for the center to see how far it has moved: center fixes are crucial for helping forecasters judge where a storm is headed. Dennis's western side is over the Gulf Stream and presumably picking up energy there, but the eye remains farther out in the Atlantic. Marks fears a landfall in North Carolina the following day.

On the way home we make a point of firing off some AXBTs and GPS sondes as close to ground-based measurement stations and buoys as we can, so that the scientists can make cross-checks of the instruments' performance. By the time we touch down at MacDill, it is 10:24 PM. Marks seems more pleased with the day's work than exhausted by the nearly nine-hour journey.

The next day we rise to learn that Dennis has veered slightly eastward, moving parallel to the Gulf Stream. The churning that cooled the sea surface, along with Dennis's failure to pass right over the Gulf Stream, means that it will not turn into the nightmare storm it might have. Yet it has yielded a treasure trove of information.

The radiometer data are the main prize. But the happy conjunction of *Miss Piggy*'s flight and D'Asaro's floats have made it a scientific field day in other respects, too. We had launched 30 GPS sondes, several of them right into Dennis's eye wall. We had also fired off 15 operative AXBTs; three of these splashed on the east-west line south of the eye where D'Asaro's floats were at work. The Doppler radar data are adequate for most purposes. In addition, Ed Walsh of the National Aeronautics and Space Administration successfully used a scanning radar altimeter during the flight to bring in a good haul of measurements on the direction and height of Dennis's waves. They are highly asymmetric and resemble a pattern Walsh saw earlier in Hurricane Bonnie.

All this information will be grist for hurricane modelers' data mills for years to come. No single storm will answer all the questions about hurricane evolution. But Marks and his crew of technicians and investigators have shown that they can deploy a comprehensive array of high-tech instruments in a dangerous cyclone and emerge with valuable results. As long as they and other riders on the storm are willing to continue risking life and limb for science, the mystery of what makes a hurricane intensify seems likely to diminish—and with it, the opportunities for some future tempest to turn without warning into a killer.

As you just read, scientists studying storms have primarily focused on wind and water activity. There also have been a number of studies in recent years on lightning. Not much data, however, exists on a puzzling phenomenon that occurs high above storms. In this region, another type of lightning strikes. Lightning is a flash of light resulting from discharges of atmospheric electricity. We are accustomed to viewing lightning in the sky, but the lightning above storms occurs in a part of the earth's atmosphere called the ionosphere. The word derives from "ionization," or "ions." Ionization is the process by which a substance breaks down into ions. Ions, in turn, are atoms that carry either a positive or a negative electrical charge.

Because they carry charges, ions can be unstable. A collection of charged ions can, at times, release the held electrical energy way up in the atmosphere. Sometimes the naked eye can see this as a dim red light above storm clouds, but usually special equipment is required to view the various types of electrical activity in the ionosphere. Future studies may reveal whether the activity somehow helps or hinders storm formation. —JV

"Lightning Between Earth and Space"
by Stephen B. Mende, Davis D. Sentman, and Eugene M. Wescott
Scientific American, August 1997

Since ancient times, lightning has both awed and fascinated people with its splendor and might. The early Greeks, for instance, associated the lightning bolt with Zeus, their most powerful god. And even after a modern understanding of the electrical nature of lightning developed, certain mysteries persisted. Many observers described luminous displays flickering through the upper reaches of the night sky. Some of these curiosities could be explained as auroras or weirdly illuminated clouds, but others were more baffling. In particular, pilots flying through the darkness occasionally observed strange flashes above thunderstorms. But the scientific community largely regarded these reports as apocryphal—until 1990, when John R. Winckler and his colleagues at the University of Minnesota first captured one of these enigmatic phantoms using a video camera. Their images revealed a lighting of a completely new configuration.

Winckler's achievement ushered in a flurry of activity to document such high-altitude electrical phenomena. And hundreds of similar observations—from the space shuttle, from aircraft and from the ground—have since followed. The result has been a growing appreciation that lightninglike effects are not at all restricted to the lower atmospheric layers sandwiched between storm clouds and the ground. Indeed, scientists now realize that electrical discharges take place regularly in the rarefied air up to 90 kilometers above thunderclouds.

It is a remarkable that these events, many of which are visible to the naked eye, went undiscovered for so long. In retrospect, the existence of some form of lightning high in the atmosphere should not have come as a surprise to scientists. They have long known that well above the turbulent parts of the atmosphere, ultraviolet rays from the sun strike gas molecules and knock electrons loose from them. This process forms the ionosphere, an electrically conducive layer that encircles the earth. Large differences in voltage can exist between storm clouds and the ionosphere, just as they do between clouds and the ground. Impelled by such enormous voltages, lightning can invade either zone when the air—which is typically an electrical insulator—breaks down and provides a conducive path for electric currents to follow.

Because the atmosphere becomes less dense with increasing altitude, the lightning that happens at greater heights involves fewer air molecules and produces colors not seen in typical discharges. Usually they appear red and are only faintly visible. Thus, researchers must employ sensitive video cameras to record these events against the backdrop of the darkened night sky. The feebleness of the light

Lightning (*left*) usually carries negative charge from the base of a cloud down to the earth. Sometimes powerful strokes (*center*) cause the positive charge that had built up near the top of the cloud to disappear abruptly. The large electrical field (*gradation in color*) created between the cloud top and the ionosphere pulls electrons upward, where they collide with gas molecules. If the electrical field is sufficiently strong and the air is sufficiently thin, the electrons will accelerate unimpeded and reach the velocity needed to transfer their kinetic energy to electronic structure of the molecules with which they collide, raising such molecules to an "excited state." The excited molecules give away their newly acquired energy by the emission of light, causing sprites (*right*). They typically span from 50 to 90 kilometers altitude.

given off and the transient nature of such emissions combine to present severe technical challenges to the researchers involved in studying these ghostly atmospheric events. Nevertheless, in just a few years investigators have made considerable progress in understanding them.

Two of us (Sentman and Wescott) have mounted airborne research campaigns using especially outfitted jets. All three of us (and many others) have also studied high-altitude electrical activity from the ground: for example, we gather every year at the invitation of Walter A. Lyons, a scientitst at ASTER in Fort Collins, Colo., and set up our equipments in his backyard laboratory—a site that offers an unobstructed view of the night sky over the thunderstorms of the Great Plains. Umran S. Inan and his colleagues at Stanford University have also recorded low-frequency radio waves from Lyon's home, measurements that have helped them to formulate theoretical models.

The newly discovered electrical events of the upper atmosphere fall into four categories. Two types of high-level lightning, termed sprites and elves, appear (despite their fanciful names) to be manifestations of well-understood atmospheric physics. The causes for the other two varieties, called blue jets and gamma-ray events, remain more speculative. But our research group and many others around the world are still amassing our observations in hopes of deciphering the physical mechanisms driving these strange occurrences as well. Until that

Electromagnetic pulses given off by strong lightning discharges create elves. Such a pulse, which is in essence an intense burst of radio static, propagates at the speed of light in all directions away from a lightning bolt. When the upward-going part of the pulse (*spherical shells*) reaches a critical height in the atmosphere (about 75 to 1000 kilometers), the electrical field it carries accelerates electrons with a great efficiency. These electrons strike air molecules, knocking them into an excited state that allows release of light. This mechanism generates expanding rings of light along the intersection of the spherical pulse with the critical layer. This intersection widens so quickly (in fact, faster than the speed of light) that these expanding rings appear as flattened disks.

time, we must admit something like the ancient sense of awe and wonder when we contemplate these curious burst of energy that dance through the ethereal world between earth and space.

The Authors

Stephen B. Mende, Davis D. Sentman, and Eugene M. Wescott have spent much of their time during recent years investigating curious electrical activity of the upper atmosphere. Mende received a Ph.D. in physics from Imperial College at the University of London in 1965. From 1967 to 1996 he worked for Lockheed Palo Alto Research Laboratory. Mende is currently a fellow at the space sciences laboratory of the University of California, Berkeley. Sentman studied space physics under James Van Allen at the University of Iowa where he earned his doctorate in 1976. After 14 years at the University of California, Los Angeles, Sentman joined the physics department at the University of Alaska–Fairbanks, where he now serves on the faculty. Wescott received a Ph.D. in geophysics from the University of Alaska–Fairbanks in 1964. He worked for three years at the National Aeronautics and Space Administration Goddard Space Flight Center in Maryland before returning to the University of Alaska–Fairbanks as a professor of geophysics.

The team of scientists who wrote the following article explain their theory on how lasers might, in the future, be used as high-tech lightning rods to divert and diminish the strength of lightning bolts. Common sense tells most of us to stay out of harm's way during strong electrical storms, but it is next to impossible to move fixed buildings that are at risk. As the authors suggest, nuclear power plants, airports, and space launch centers can sustain incredible damage if hit by lightning. Lasers might one day automatically scan over these facilities to safeguard them from lightning strikes.

The proposed system works by ionizing air. To ionize means to split off one or more electrons from an atom, which leaves the atom with a positive electronic charge. When ultraviolet light is used to promote this activity, ionization occurs along a straight path, according to the authors who developed the system. Since lightning travels along such paths, the system, at least in theory and in experiments, controls where lightning will strike. —JV

"Lightning Control with Lasers"
by Jean-Claude Diels, Ralph Bernstein, Karl E. Stahlkopf, and Xin Miao Zhao
Scientific American, August 1997

Despite centuries of scientific scrutiny—including Benjamin Franklin's famous experiment with a kite—lightning has remained a strangely mysterious phenomenon. Although scientists from Franklin's time onward have understood that electrical charges can slowly accumulate in clouds and then create brilliant flashes when the stored energy suddenly discharges, they puzzled for years over the exact physical mechanisms governing this process. How quickly do lightning strokes travel? What determines the path the energy takes? What happens to the bolt of electric current after it penetrates the ground? Such questions eventually yielded to scientific investigation. And this research has not only expanded the fundamental understanding of lightning, it has raised the prospect of exerting control over where lightning strikes—something traditionally considered a matter of divine whim.

Although lightning is inherently erratic, its aggregate effect is enormous. Every year in the U.S. (where about 20 million individual flashes hit the ground), lightning kills several hundred people and causes extensive property damage, including forest fires. Lightning is also responsible for about half the power failures in areas prone to thunderstorms, costing electric utility companies in this country perhaps as much as $1 billion annually in damaged equipment and lost revenue. Lightning can also disrupt the navigational devices on commercial airliners (or even on rockets bound for space), and it has caused one serious malfunction at a nuclear power plant.

So it is no wonder that people have sought ways to prevent lightning from doing harm. Unlike the ancients who tried to protect themselves by offering sacrifices to the gods, scientists and engineers have come up with solutions that have proved moderately successful.

People can often avoid the worst effects of lightning by mounting well-grounded lightning rods on buildings, as first suggested by Franklin soon after he reeled in his experimental kite in 1752. Although he initially believed that such pointed rods worked because "the electrical fire would . . . be drawn out of the cloud silently, before it could come near enough to strike," Franklin later realized that these devices either channel the discharge or work to direct lightning away. This same principle—to divert rather than to prevent a strike—provides the basis for currently used methods of protection (such as lightning arrestors or grounded shielding) as well as our own efforts toward controlling lightning with lasers.

Locating the Problem

Beginning in the late 1970s, researchers at the State University of New York at Albany established a small network of direction-finding antennas that served to track cloud-to-ground lightning strikes over a limited area of their state. Throughout the 1980s, that network of specialized detectors slowly expanded to include other states, and by 1991 (the year commercial operations started), this group of specialized antennas could sense the occurrence of lightning anywhere in the country.

That vast array, now known as the National Lightning Detection Network, consists of about 100 stations that monitor lightning by sensing the exact timing and direction of the bursts of electromagnetic energy given off by these discharges. The stations relay their many measurements through communications satellites to a control center in Tucson, Ariz., where a computer processes this information and continually disseminates reports about lightning activity. Hundreds of subscribers benefit from this service, including various electric utility companies, airlines and even the U.S. Strategic Air Command. The managers of some electric utilities, for example, have been able to save more than half a million dollars annually by using this information to dispatch repair crews swiftly to sites where lightning might soon strike or where it has already damaged the lines. But the people who oversee particularly sensitive installations—including nuclear power plants and electric power substations—await even more sophisticated methods to make lightning less of a threat.

Efforts to satisfy that need include research being conducted at a unique field laboratory near Starke, Fla. In 1993 two of us (Bernstein and Stahlkopf), along with other members of the Electric Power Research Institute in Palo Alto, Calif., arranged for Power Technologies in Schenectady, N.Y., to build a special facility at the Camp Blanding Florida National Guard station to test the susceptibility of various underground and overhead structures to damage from lightning. Rather than waiting for a chance strike, researchers working at this field site (which is now operated by the University of Florida) can trigger lightning using small rockets that trail a thin, grounded wire.

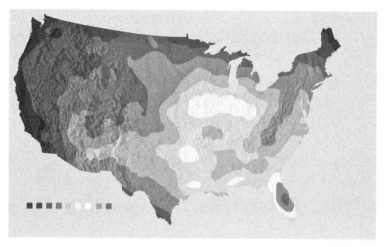

National Lightning Detection Network, which is now run by Global Atmospherics in Tucson, Ariz., monitors lightning activity across the U.S., where the density of lightning flashes varies enormously. By tracking the timing and direction of electromagnetic pulses given off by lightning, this network of sensors can pinpoint the location of individual flashes and estimate their magnitudes.

Unlike such triggered discharges, a natural lightning bolt begins with a barely visible precursor, called the leader phase, which propagates downward from the cloud toward the ground in stepwise fashion, knocking electrons loose from molecules of atmospheric gas along the way and creating a channel of ionized air that then serves as a conductive conduit. Immediately after the leader phase connects with the ground, the bright and energetic "return phase" erupts. As happens during the leader phase, the return stroke, which carries currents that range from a few thousand amperes up to about 300,000 amperes (household wiring typically carries no more than a few tens of amperes), is driven by the tremendous voltage potential—hundreds of millions of volts—between the ground and the thunderclouds overhead. This dazzling bolt travels at speeds that can approach half the speed of light, and the huge electric current it carries with it can easily destroy an object caught in its path.

Averting Catastrophe

Just as rockets trailing grounded wires represent a modern version of Franklin's kite experiment, we believe that in the near future laser beams may serve as high-tech lightning rods, offering a way to divert lightning from especially critical sites where it might do great harm. Decades ago some forward thinking people envisioned using lasers to trigger lightning by creating an electrically conductive channel of ionized air. But their attempts—including some that employed the most intense lasers available—were unsuccessful. Those lasers ionized the air so thoroughly as to make it essentially opaque to the beam, which then could not penetrate any farther.

Two teams of Japanese scientists have recently endeavored to overcome this difficulty by using powerful infrared lasers. Rather than trying to create a continuous channel of ionized particles, these scientists have worked out a way to focus one or more laser beams at successively displaced points so as to create a dotted line of separate plasma bubbles along the intended path of the lightning bolt. They have achieved a controlled discharge more than seven meters long in laboratory tests. Still, they were able to achieve that feat only with extreme electrical fields, when the air was already close to the point of breaking down spontaneously.

Two of us (Diels and Zhao) have explored another approach that uses ultraviolet light from a relatively low energy laser. At first glance, this technique does not seem at all promising. Such beams do not ionize the air molecules in their paths particularly effectively, and the few negatively charged electrons that are shaken loose by the ultraviolet light quickly combine with neutral oxygen molecules nearby, forming negative oxygen ions (which reduce the conductivity of the channel). Nevertheless, this method can produce uniform ionization along an extended straight path. That ionized line then acts much as a lightning rod, concentrating the electrical field so intensely at its tip that the air ahead breaks down and adds more length to the conductive path.

We have also found that directing a second visible-light laser along the path of the ultraviolet beam counteracts the tendency for free electrons to attach to neutral oxygen molecules, forming negative oxygen ions. This tactic works because photons of the visible-light beam carry sufficient energy to knock electrons free from the negative ions.

Although the ultraviolet laser we have tested operates at low power levels overall, it ionizes air surprisingly well. The key is to use extremely short laser pulses. The brief duration of these bursts (less than a trillionth of a second) makes it possible for the laser light to have high peak intensity, although the average power consumed by the apparatus is quite modest. What is more, we can take advantage of the physics of laser propagation in air and impart a particular shape to the pulses emitted by the laser. The pulses will then tend to compress as they propagate through the atmosphere. The higher energies jammed into these compact packages of light compensate for energy lost along the way from scattering or absorption.

Although we have not yet tried to trigger lightning in this way, the agreement of our theoretical calculations, numerical simulations and small-scale laboratory experiments makes us confident that we are well on the way. We have, for example, succeeded in using short pulses of ultraviolet laser light to create a conductive channel between two highly charged electrodes spaced 25 centimeters apart. The lasers are able to trigger an electrical discharge when the voltage difference between the electrodes is less than half of what is normally required for the air to break down. That is, we can force laboratory scale lightning to form along a prescribed channel well in advance of the point that a discharge would spontaneously occur.

Moving Outdoors

With the help of Patrick Rambo, our colleague at the University of New Mexico, we have recently built an ultraviolet laser that is 100 times more powerful than

Laser diversion of lightning might take various forms. Engineers initially imagined that powerful infrared lasers could produce a conductive path in the sky, but these beams completely ionized the air in front of them, which then becomes opaque and scatters the light (*a*). Researchers in Japan are experimenting with multiple beams that are focused using a series of mirrors to form a line of ionized pockets that should help channel a lightning bolt (*b*). The authors' method relies on paired ultra-violet and visible-light laser beams (aimed upward with a single mirror), which should be able to form a straight path of ionization for lighting to follow (*c*). Grounded rods would interrupt the resulting lightning strike, protecting the mirror and the laser apparatus. Alternatively, the beam could be arranged to graze a tall grounded mast as it shoots skyward.

any we have previously tested. We plan to fire this laser 10 times each second during a thunderstorm. Although we are anxious to see just how effective such a laser can be, we have not yet arranged the proper preliminary tests, which require a special high-voltage facility, such as the one operated by Mississippi State University.

Unfortunately, our laser is too delicate and cumbersome to move across the country. But we hope soon to complete a mobile ultraviolet laser, which (when coupled to a suitable visible-light laser) should be able to trigger laboratory discharges many meters long. Perhaps the same laser pair will finally provide the means to set off lightning from clouds—an accomplishment that has so far eluded our various competitors working with other types of lasers.

If any of these approaches to sparking lightning with laser beams ultimately succeeds, application of the technique could be commonplace. Lasers might one day scan the skies over nuclear power plants, airports and space launch centers. And electric utilities of the 21st century, with their growing network of equipment at risk, may finally acquire the means to act on the threat of a gathering storm, instead of being destined to react only after the damage is done.

The Authors

Jean-Claude Diels, Ralph Bernstein, Karl E. Stahlkopf, and Xin Miao Zhao became involved in lightning diversion for somewhat different reasons. Diels, a professor in the department of physics and astronomy at the University of New Mexico, and Zhao, a researcher at Los Alamos National Laboratory, began working together in 1990 with "ultrafast" pulsed lasers and quickly saw the possibility of using such devices to control lightning. After two years of further research, they received a patent for their invention. Bernstein, a project manager at the Electric Power Research Institute, and Stahlkopf, a vice president working with him, both trained as electrical engineers; they earned, respectively, a master's degree from Syracuse University and a doctorate from the University of California, Berkeley. Their wish to speed the development of technologies to lessen the damage from lightning motivated them to provide funding for lightning detection, rocket-triggered lightning experiments and, most recently, lightning control with lasers.

In the popular movie The Wizard of Oz, a tornado hits Kansas and results in the injury of the main character, Dorothy. While the movie is fiction, tornadoes, particularly in the state of Kansas, present a real threat. Almost every year, tornadoes affect the state. A tornado is a whirling wind that forms a vortex and can travel quickly over land.

Like a hurricane, a tornado has a central "cell" region, only it is usually described as a supercell because the dense wall of clouds pack tightly together in less space. Tornadoes, therefore, are usually smaller than hurricanes, in terms of the land area they can cover, but they may pack *a stronger punch because their energy is so condensed.*

Researchers follow tornadoes, as they do hurricanes, but they usually do it on land in specially equipped vehicles, as presented in the following article. They often use Doppler weather radar, just as the hurricane chasers do, to measure wind speeds and moisture levels from a safe distance. The radar technique has been utilized since the early 1970s, but improvements have led to greater accuracy. In the future, scientists hope to learn whether observed cloud changes can help them predict tornado formation. —JV

"Tornadoes"
by Robert Davies-Jones
Scientific American, August 1995

This spring was a frenzied tornado season in the U.S. In May alone, an estimated 484 tornadoes killed some 16 people and ravaged millions of dollars of property. Day after day, forecasts of severe storms sent me and my colleagues rushing from the National Severe Storms Laboratory (NSSL) in Norman, Okla., to Texas or Kansas, returning sometimes at three in the morning. After the day's briefing at 9 AM, we might set off again, fatigued but hoping once more to collect precious data on the birth of tornadoes.

On Tuesday, May 16, the weather maps revealed the threat of afternoon tornadoes in Kansas. By 5 PM a menacing thunderstorm had erupted, fed by warm, moist southerly winds that rose and rotated in an updraft. The storm was a highly organized "supercell," an ideal tornado breeding ground. As William Gargan, a graduate student at the University of Oklahoma, and I approached from the southeast in our instrumented car, called Probe 1, we glimpsed the 10-mile high top of the monstrous storm 60 miles away. The thunderstorm was sweeping east-northeast at 30 miles per hour, quite typical motion in the Great Plains.

As we closed to within 10 miles along Route 50, we saw for the first time the long, dark cloud base. Within a few miles we spotted a twister, shaped like an elephant's trunk, hanging from the rear of the main cloud tower, near Garden City. In trying to maneuver closer on minor paved roads, we lost sight of the twister but spied it again four miles to our northwest. It was thin and trailed horizontally behind its parent cloud before bending abruptly toward the ground at a right angle. Clearly, it was being pushed away from the cloud by the cold air flowing down from the storm, and nearing the end of its life.

Supercells

Most tornadoes have damage paths 150 feet wide, move at about 30 miles per hour and last only a few minutes. Extremely destructive ones may be over a mile wide, travel at 60 miles per hour and may be on the ground for more than an hour. Tornadoes in the Northern Hemisphere, such as the devastating ones that occur in the U.S., northeastern India and Bangladesh, nearly always rotate counterclockwise when viewed from above. Southern Hemisphere tornadoes, such as those that form in Australia, tend to rotate clockwise. These directions are called cyclonic.

In 1949 Edward M. Brooks of St. Louis University discovered, by examining how air pressure changes at weather stations near tornadoes, that the twisters usually form within larger masses of rotating air known as mesocyclones. In 1953 a mesocyclone appeared on a radar screen at Urbana, Ill., as a hook-shaped appendage on the southwest side of a storm's radar echo. Because rain reflects the microwaves emitted by radar, the hook shape indicated that the rain was being drawn into a cyclonically rotating curtain. And in 1957 T. Theodore Fujita of the University of Chicago examined photographs and movies taken by local residents of the base and sides of a North Dakota tornadic storm and found that the entire cloud tower was rotating cyclonically.

In the 1960s Keith A. Browning, a British meteorologist visiting the NSSL's precursor, the National Severe Storms Project, pieced together from radar data a remarkably accurate picture of tornadic storms. He realized that most tornadoes are spawned inside particularly large and vicious storms that he dubbed supercells. These powerful systems develop in very unstable environments in which the winds vary markedly with height and cool, dry air lies atop warm, moist air about a mile deep over the earth's surface.

Anatomy of a Tornadic Storm

A supercell thunderstorm erupts when warm, moist air breaks through an overlaying stable layer and moves upward through cool, dry air. In the Northern Hemisphere, the updraft is tilted to the northeast and rotates anti-clockwise when viewed from above. The warm air parcels decelerate in the stratosphere, fall back down and spread sideways in the "anvil." In the northeast part of the storm, rain falls out of the tilted updraft into mid-level dry air, cooling it and causing it to sink. The supercell's rotation pulls some of the rain and the cool air around to the southwest side of the storm. Near the ground, warm air and rain-cooled air meet in a turbulent boundary called the gust front. Lowered wall clouds and tornadoes tend to form along this line, near a cusp marking the storm's center of rotation.

A thin stable layer separates the two air masses, bottling up the instability.

This lid can be pried open if the low-level air is warmed by the sun or if a weather system invades. Fronts, jet streams and upper-level disturbances, common visitors to the Great Plains during tornado season, all may force low-level air upward. Because air pressure falls with height, the rising parcels of air expand and cool. At sufficient height they become cold enough that their water vapor starts to condense into misty droplets, forming a flat cloud base.

In condensing, the vapor releases latent heat, warming the air parcels. They reach a level at which they become warmer than their environment and rise freely to great heights at speeds up to 150 miles per hour, forming a towering thunderhead. Shearing winds tilt the updraft to the northeast.

As they ascend, cloud droplets coalesce into raindrops. The buoyancy of the air parcels is partly offset by the weight of their own water and ice. The parcels lose momentum in the stratosphere, sink down to about eight miles and flow out sideways, forming the storm's "anvil." Rain falling out of the tilted updraft evaporates in dry, mid-level air on the northeast side of the supercell, causing this air to cool and sink to the earth. With time the rain and cool downdraft are pulled around the updraft by the storm's rotation. The cool air has higher relative humidity than the warm air and if forced upward becomes cloudy at lesser heights. Thus, when some of this air is sucked into the updraft, lowered wall cloud forms.

In contrast with most thunderstorms, which contain several updrafts and downdrafts that interfere with one another, supercells contain one or two cells, each with its own coexisting downdraft and broad rotating updraft. The high level of organization allows a supercell to live a long time in an almost steady and intense state that is conducive to tornado formation. A region of updraft one to three miles in radius may begin to rotate with wind speeds of 50 miles per hour or more, forming a mesocyclone. The storm may then develop low-level rotation and even a tornado—usually to the southwest side of the updraft and close to an adjacent downdraft, while the mesocyclone is mature or decaying.

Ultimately, the mesocyclone dies in a shroud of rain as its updraft is cut off near the earth's surface by very cold air flowing out of the heart of the downdraft. In persistent supercells, a new mesocyclone may have already formed a few miles southeast of the dying one, along the gust front—the boundary between the warm and cool air. A new tornado may develop rapidly.

Tornado Chasing

To pin down when and where a twister is most likely to appear, the NSSL conducted a Tornado Intercept Project from 1972 to 1986. The intercept teams initially acquired film footage for measuring extreme wind speeds and provided "ground truth" for radar observations. But other benefits ensued. The chasers observed that tornadoes often develop in parts of a storm that are free of rain and lightning, eliminating theories that relied on these stimuli to trigger tornadoes. And in 1975 a rare anticyclonic tornado was recorded. Its rotation, being opposite to that of the earth, was not simply an amplification of the planet's spin.

During the past two springs, the NSSL has been hosting another project, the Verification of the Origins of Rotation in Tornadoes Experiment (VORTEX). Measurements are being made in and near supercells by an armada of vehicles. One of these vans is piloted by the field coordinator, Erik N. Rasmussen of the NSSL, who works with meteorologists at headquarters in Norman to choose a target storm and coordinate the entire data collection. Five vans are equipped to obtain upper-air balloon soundings in and near storms, and 12 others have weather stations mounted on their roofs. These instruments are supported 10 feet above the

Destructive Power

The damage that tornadoes inflict on buildings . . . and the distances that they carry heavy objects reveal the extreme wind speeds attained near the ground. In the 1970s the Institute for Disaster Research in Lubbock, Tex., concluded that the worst damage required winds of up to 275 miles per hour. The engineers also noted that windward walls of buildings, generally to the southwest, almost always fall inward—implying that structures are most often damaged by the brute force of a wind, not by the sudden drop in atmospheric pressure. As a result, residents of "Tornado Alley," in the midwestern U.S., were no longer advised to open windows to reduce the pressure inside. The suggestion had caused many people to be cut by flying glass as they rushed to open the windows. Nor were residents told anymore to hide in the southwest corner of the house—where they were in the most danger of having walls fall in on them. Now residents are urged to shelter in a central closet because of the added protection of interior walls.

ground well above the vehicles' slipstream, with the data being stored and displayed on laptop computers inside.

One of these 12 cars aims to obtain film footage of tornadoes for analysis; two others deploy nine Turtles. Named thus because they resemble sea turtles in shape, Turtles are 40-pound instrument packages that are designed to withstand a tornado. They have well-shielded sensors to measure temperature and pressure and are placed on the ground ahead of tornadoes, at 100-yard intervals.

The remaining nine vans are called Probes; their sole mission is to collect weather data in specified regions of the storm. Probe 1's mission is to measure temperature gradients close to and north of the tornado or mesocyclone, a region where large hail frequently falls. Twice this season softball-size hail has smashed Probe 1's windshield.

That Tuesday in Kansas, as the twister died, we raced eastward to stay abreast of the storm and find a new mesocyclone. As we zigzagged in rain along the gravel roads, we encountered two rows of up to eight power poles that were lying in the fields, snapped off two feet above the ground. There must have been a strong tornado hidden in the rain to our northeast. (The next day I read in the newspaper that 150 poles had been downed.)

About 30 miles further east, we spotted a wall cloud, a rotating, pedestal-like lowering, a few miles across, of the main cloud base. A narrow tornado appeared, not out of the dark wall cloud as is usual but from an adjacent higher cloud base. This vortex touched down briefly, raising debris, but lived out its few minutes of existence mainly as a funnel cloud aloft, without visible signs of contact with the ground.

A new wall cloud, which became ominously large and low, developed to the northeast. That, however, failed to produce a tornado. Near Jetmore, a fresh storm developed to the south of the one we were following. We went north to confirm that this older storm was indeed losing its tornado potential, then retraced our path and dropped south to the new one.

Signature of a Vortex

In addition to the aforementioned armada, VORTEX also uses two airplanes flying around a storm, as well as three more vehicles. All of these deploy Doppler radar, instruments that yield vital information about the airflow in tornadic storms. The newest, mobile Doppler radar, built this year by Joshua Wurman and Jerry M. Straka of the University of Oklahoma, has already yielded unprecedented details of tornadoes.

Doppler weather radars measure wind speeds from afar by emitting pulses of microwave radiation and catching their reflections off a group of raindrops or ice particles. If the drops are moving toward the radar, the reflected pulse has a shorter wavelength that betrays this component of the drops' velocity. (State troopers use similar instruments to catch speeding cars.)

The first Doppler measurements in 1971 confirmed that the winds within a "hook" are indeed rotating, at speeds of about 50 miles per hour. This circulation, first apparent at a height of about three miles, is followed by rotation at much lower levels, preceding the development of any intense tornado. In 1973 a small anomaly on the Doppler velocity map of a tornadic storm at Union City, Okla., turned out to coincide in time and space with a violent tornado.

The radar could not "see" or resolve the tornado directly but showed high winds changing direction abruptly across the twister and its precursor in the clouds. This vortex signature typically forms at around 9,000 feet 10 to 20 minutes before touchdown. It may extend upward as well as downward, occasionally reaching seven miles high for large tornadoes.

Although the vortex signature can be used to warn the public to seek shelter in a basement or an interior closet, it can be observed only at quite close range, generally 60 miles or less. At longer ranges of up to 150 miles, tornado warnings can be issued on the basis of Doppler radar detection of the parent mesocyclone. Federal agencies are currently installing a network of sophisticated Doppler radars across the country to improve warning capabilities.

In 1991, using a portable Doppler radar near a tumultuous tornado at Red Rock, Okla., Howard B. Bluestein of Oklahoma University measured wind speeds of up to 280 miles per hour. Although high, these speeds are a far cry from the 500 miles per hour postulated 40 years ago to explain freak happenings such as pieces of straw stuck in trees. (A more likely explanation for this phenomenon is that the wind forces apart the wood grains, which then snap shut, trapping the straw.)

Individual Doppler radar suffices for local warnings, but a second Doppler device that is about 25 to 35 miles away and views a storm from a significantly different angle supplies a far more complete picture for research. Such a dual-Doppler system, used by the NSSL and others since 1974, measures the velocity of the rain in two different directions. Knowing that the mass of air is conserved, and estimating the speed with which rain is falling relative to the moving air, meteorologists can reconstruct the three-dimensional wind field and compute quantities such as vorticity (or local spin in the air). Such data have led them to discover that a tornado is located to one side of its parent updraft, near a downdraft, and to verify that air flowing into a mesocyclone spins about its direction of motion.

Spinning Up

A major breakthrough in understanding the complex rotations in tornadic storms came in 1978, when computer simulations made by Robert Wilhelmson of the University of Illinois and Joseph B. Klemp of the National Center for Atmospheric Research (NCAR) reproduced realistic supercells complete with such features as hook-shaped precipitation patterns. Proceeding in small time steps, the scientists numerically solved the equations governing temperature, wind velocity and conservation of mass for air and water in various forms—vapor, cloud droplets and raindrops—on a three-dimensional array of points emulating space.

In the simulated world at least, scientists were in control. Even without any lateral variations in the initial environment, they were able to create supercells, thereby debunking the popular explanation that tornadoes are caused by colliding air masses. And by "turning off" the earth's rotation, they established that it had little effect during the first few hours of a storm's life. Rather wind direction that at low levels veered with height was crucial to the development of rotation.

In a typical supercell environment the wind near the ground is from the southeast, the wind half a mile above the ground is from the south, and the wind one mile high is from the southwest. Wind that changes speed or direction with height also contains spin. Envision how the wind would make an initially vertical stick rotate: if a south wind blows slowly near the ground and faster higher up, the stick will spin about an east-west axis.

But what if the wind, instead of changing speed, changes direction from southeast to southwest? Imagine the stick moving north, along with the mid-level wind, half a mile up. Then its top is pushed eastward and its bottom westward, so that it will turn about a north-south axis. Therefore, this air has "streamwise" vorticity—it spins about its direction of motion, much like a spiraling American football.

Air parcels with streamwise vorticity have their spin axes tilted upward as they enter an updraft.

Thus, the updraft as a whole rotates cyclonically. First proposed by Browning in 1963 and proved analytically in the 1980s by Douglas K. Lilly of the University of Oklahoma and me, this theory explains how the updraft rotates at mid-levels. But it does not explain how rotation develops very close to the ground. As simulations by Klemp and Richard Rotunno of NCAR showed in 1985, low-level rotation depends on the supercell's evaporatively cooled downdraft: it does not occur when the evaporation of rain is "switched off."

The simulations revealed, surprisingly, that the low-level rotation originates north of the mesocyclone, in moderately rain-cooled, subsiding air. As the mid-level rotation draws the downdraft cyclonically around the updraft, some of the downdraft's cool air travels southward with warm air on its left and much colder air on its right. Warm air, being buoyant, pulls the left sides of the air parcels upward; the cold air pulls their right sides downward. Then the cool air starts to rotate about its horizontal direction of motion. But as it descends, its spin axis is tilted downward, giving rise to anticyclonic spin.

Harold E. Brooks, also at the NSSL, and I showed in 1993 that, by a rather complex mechanism, the spin in the subsiding cool air reverses direction before the air completes its descent. Eventually, this cyclonically rotating air is present at very low levels. This moderately cool air flows along the surface and is sucked up into the southwest side of the updraft. Because the flow to the updraft is convergent, the air rotates faster, like

Tabletop Tornado

Laboratory experiments have helped explain why tornadoes can take different forms. In the apparatus built in the 1960s by Neil B. Ward of the National Severe Storms Laboratory in Norman, Okla., and refined by John T. Snow and others at Purdue University, air is spun up by a rotating screen as it enters a lower compartment. It then flows up into the main chamber through a wide central hole, being pulled by exhaust fans at the top. The device has replicated many features of real tornadoes, such as the pattern of air pressures near the lower surface.

Reinterpreting Ward's results, I found in 1973 that the crucial parameter for tornado formation is the swirl ratio S, first used by W. Stephen Lewellen of West Virginia University. S is the ratio of the tangential velocity at the edge of the updraft hole (controlled by the screen's rotation) to the average upward velocity through the hole (determined by the fan). For S less than 0.1, there is no vortex. As S is increased, a vortex appears, having an intense upward jet at low levels. At S higher than 0.45, the vortex becomes fully turbulent with a central downdraft surrounded by a strong updraft. And at a critical swirl ratio of roughly 1.0, a pair of vortices form on opposite sides of the parent vortex. For still higher swirl ratios, up to six subsidiary vortices have been observed.

an ice skater who spins more rapidly by drawing in her arms.

Despite understanding well how large-scale rotation develops at middle and low levels of a mesocyclone, we have yet to pin down why tornadoes are formed. The simplest explanation is that they are the result of surface friction. This observation seems paradoxical because friction generally reduces wind speeds. But the net effect of friction is much like that in a stirred cup of tea.

Drag does reduce speeds and therefore centrifugal forces in a thin layer near the bottom. It causes the fluid to move inward along the cup's base, as made apparent by tea leaves bunching up at the center. But fluid near the top of this inflow spins faster as it falls in toward the axis because of the ice-skater effect. The result is a vortex along the axis of the cup. W. Stephen Lewellen of West Virginia University concludes that the highest wind speeds in a tornado are located in the lowest 300 feet.

Friction also explains the persistence of twisters. A tornado has a partial vacuum in its core; centrifugal forces prevent the air from spiraling inward through the sides of the tornado. In 1969 Bruce R. Morton of Monash University in Australia explained how the vacuum survives. Strong buoyancy forces prevent air from entering the core through the top. Close to the ground, friction reduces tangential velocity and hence centrifugal forces, allowing a strong but shallow inflow into the core. But friction also acts to limit the inflow winds, not allowing enough air in to fill up the core. Tornadoes intensify and become more stable after they make strong contact with the ground because their inflows become restricted to a thin boundary layer.

The friction theory does not explain, however, why a tornadic vortex signature up in the clouds sometimes foreshadows the touchdown of a tornado by 10 to 20 minutes.

Touchdown

Many of the classic features of tornadoes were unexpectedly demonstrated to us on that May day in Kansas. By the time we had moved to the southern storm in the small town of Hanston, it was getting dark, and operations were ending. But then the field coordinator advised the teams of a rapidly rotating wall cloud in our vicinity. As the warning sirens started wailing, we watched a skinny, serpentine tornado touch down three miles to our southeast.

We took off to the north to place ourselves ahead of the tornado, unaware in the excitement of a deep drainage ditch in the street. It damaged our wheel and tilted our weather station, but we kept going. We turned on to a dirt road to take us east on the north side of the tornado, which had now become a wide column of dust with a bowl-shaped lowering of the cloud base above it. As we got ahead of the tornado, it transformed itself into several smaller vortices, all circling furiously around the tornado's central axis. (In 1967 Fujita observed that some tornadoes left behind beheaded cornstalks in several overlapping swaths. Neil B. Ward of the NSSL later attributed these curious patterns to such subsidiary twisters. Like a point on the rim of a bicycle wheel that circles the center as the wheel moves forward, these frenetic subvortices trace out cycloidal paths.)

Low on gas, we raced ahead of the twister, apprehensive because we did not know if and where the road ended. The tornado was perhaps a mile away and not moving perceptibly across our field of view, indicating that it was heading directly for us at 30 miles per hour. The field coordinator came to our rescue by informing us of a road north, toward Burdett, which we gratefully took. We stopped after a mile to watch the tornado, which had been on the ground for at least 14 miles and now had a classic stovepipe appearance, pass by to our south and recede into the darkness to our east.

We limped home, our car damaged, our data uncertain and our pulses racing, buoyed by the news that great radar data had been obtained from the air and from the new portable ground radar. Looking back, we should have just kept pace with the tornado instead of passing it and turning ourselves, the hunters, into the hunted.

The Author

Robert Davies-Jones studies the dynamics and genesis of tornadoes at the National Severe Storms Laboratory (NSSL) in Norman, Okla. He is also an adjunct professor of meteorology at the University of Oklahoma. After earning a B.Sc. in physics from the University of Birmingham in England, he studied the sun's convection at the University of Colorado, obtaining a Ph.D. in astro-geophysics in 1969. A year later he joined the NSSL, this time applying his knowledge of fluid dynamics to the weather. He serves as co-chief editor of the Journal of the Atmospheric Sciences.

4 Asteroid Impacts

The following article begins with the sentence, "By now it is common knowledge that the impact of an asteroid or comet brought the age of the dinosaurs to an abrupt end." It then goes on to explain that the collision ignited global wildfires, destroying ecosystems and generating other environmental catastrophes. It also presents a theory of how life on the planet rebounded.

While the asteroid theory is common knowledge, many researchers, particularly in recent years, have disagreed with the theory. Another theory, supported by fossils and other archaeological evidence, holds that dinosaurs slowly died off due to gradual climate change. Still other scientists have proposed that numerous volcanic explosions resulted in toxic gas and debris that could have wiped out the dinosaurs and other animals 65 million years ago. Dinosaur extinction remains an unsolved mystery, but the dangers associated with asteroid and other space object impacts are believed to be quite real, as you will read later in this volume. —JV

"The Day the World Burned"
by David A. Kring and Daniel D. Durda
Scientific American, December 2003

By now it is common knowledge that the impact of an asteroid or comet brought the age of the dinosaurs to an abrupt end. Less well known, though, is exactly how they and so many other species became extinct and how ecosystems managed to rebuild themselves afterward. The cataclysm went far beyond the regular insults from which living things must recover. The asteroid or comet flashed through the sky more than 40 times as fast as the speed of sound. It was so large that when its leading edge made contact with ground, its trailing edge was at least as high as the cruising altitude of a commercial airliner. It produced an explosion equivalent to 100 trillion tons of TNT, a greater release of energy than any event on our planet in the 65 million years since then.

The remnants of that collision lie below the tropical forest of the Yucatán, the Maya ruins of Mayapán, the seaport village of Progreso and the waters of the Gulf of Mexico. The crater, called Chicxulub after modern Maya villages in the area, is approximately 180 kilometers in diameter and is surrounded by a circular fault 240 kilometers across, apparently produced when the crust reverberated with the shock of the impact.

Science sometimes overwhelms science fiction in its capacity to startle and amaze. Such is the case for this impact. It destroyed one world and made way for a new one. But studies over the past several years suggest that the impact did not kill off species directly or immediately. Rather it had a variety of severe and complex environmental effects that spread the devastation worldwide. One of the most destructive forces was the ignition of vast wildfires that swept across continents. The fires wiped out critical habitats, wrecked the base of the continental food chain and contributed to a global shutdown of photosynthesis.

Broiler Oven

To see the imprint of mass death for yourself, you can visit any number of rock outcrops in the western U.S., southern Europe and elsewhere. An especially good location is the Raton Basin in Colorado and New Mexico. Sandwiched between rock layers from the Cretaceous (K) period of the dinosaurs and the subsequent Tertiary (T) period is a one-centimeter layer of clay laced with exotic elements. Looking closely at the layer in various locations around the world, Wendy S. Wolbach of DePaul University and her colleagues made a startling discovery in 1985. They found microscopic particles of soot—spherical particles of carbon often clustered like grapes, with a composition that matches the smoke from forest fires. Globally the soot amounts to nearly 70 billion tons of residue. It is the ash of the Cretaceous world.

At the time, the soot interested researchers mainly as additional evidence that the mass extinction was caused by an impact rather than by volcanoes, whose effect would not have been so abrupt or widespread [see "An Extraterrestrial Impact," by Walter Alvarez and Frank Asaro; SCIENTIFIC AMERICAN, October 1990]. In 1990 University of Arizona planetary scientist H. Jay Melosh and his colleagues described how an impact could have set off fires around the world. As it hit, the asteroid or comet disintegrated and vaporized a chunk of Earth's crust, creating a plume of debris. With increasing speed, the fiery plume rose out of the crater and rocketed through the atmosphere, carrying crystals of quartz that, only moments before, had been as deep as 10 kilometers below the surface.

The plume swelled to a diameter of 100 to 200 kilometers, punching its way into space and expanding until it enveloped the entire Earth. Material then began to fall back under the influence of gravity, plowing into the atmosphere with nearly all the energy with which it had been launched from Chicxulub. Moving at speeds of 7,000 to 40,000 kilometers an hour, the particles lit up the sky like trillions of meteors and heated a large volume of the atmosphere to several hundred degrees, before slowly settling to the ground and forming the layer we see today.

Melosh's team calculated that the reentering debris could have ignited vegetation over a huge fraction of the globe. But nobody in 1990 knew the location or precise size of the impact, so the team could not determine the total amount of heating or the distribution of the fires. Although soot had been found throughout the world, fires need not have erupted everywhere,

A World Lost, a World Remade

THE DAY BEFORE

Late Cretaceous swamps and rivers in North America had a mix of coniferous, broad-leaved evergreen and deciduous trees. They formed canopied forests and open woodlands with understories of ferns, aquatic plants and flowering shrubs.

IMPACT

The Chicxulub Impact occurred in a shallow sea and immediately lofted rocky, molten and vaporous debris into the atmosphere. The bulk of the debris rained down on nearby continental regions, but much of it rose all the way into space.

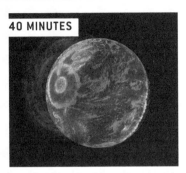

40 MINUTES

The vapor-rich plume of material expanded to envelop Earth. As material in that plume fell back to the ground, it streaked through the atmosphere like trillions of meteors, heating it in some places by hundreds of degrees.

ONE WEEK

After fires had ravaged the landscape, only a few stark trunks and skeletons remained. Soot from the fires and dust from the impact slowly settled to the ground. Sunlight was dramatically, if not totally attenuated for months.

continued on page 194

continued from page 193

ONE YEAR

The postimpact environment was less diverse. Ferns and algae were the first to recover. Plant species in swamps and swamp margins generally survived better than species in other types of ecosystems. Conifers fared particularly badly.

50 YEARS

Shrubs took advantage of the vacant landscape and began to cover it. Species pollinated by the wind did better than those that relied on insects. Trees began to grow, but it took years for forest canopies to rebuild. The recovery time is uncertain.

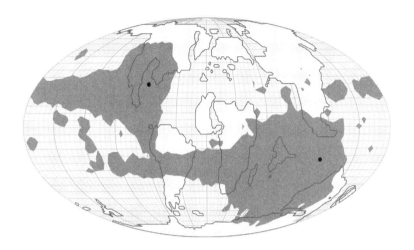

Toasted planet: To dry out plants and set them on fire takes 12,500 watts of heating per square meter for at least 20 minutes. These conditions were reached in two main areas, centered on Chicxulub and its antipode in India. From these regions, corridors of fire stretched westward as Earth rotated beneath the hail of reentering debris. This computer simulation assumes a certain impact configuration; other scenarios incinerated even larger areas.

because soot could have been blown to some sites by the wind.

A Blue Rain Doth Fall

Soon after Melosh reported his findings, a team of seven American, Canadian and Mexican scientists (including one of us, Kring) discovered that Chicxulub was the impact site. This discovery settled the argument over the root cause of the extinction. Since then, researchers' attention has turned to the details of the event.

Last year the two of us completed a new study of the wildfires. Knowledge of the impact location allowed us to reconstruct the trajectories and distribution of material ejected from the crater and evaluate the extent of the fires. Our calculations suggest that some of the material reached halfway to the moon before plummeting back to Earth. Within four days almost all of it had returned to Earth. Slightly more than 10 percent escaped Earth's gravity altogether, to be flung across the solar system and possibly to collide with other planets. (Similarly, pieces of Mars and the moon have landed on Earth, although the ejection process differed.)

The reentering debris heated the atmosphere so severely that it ignited wildfires in the southern and central areas of North America, central South America, central Africa, the Indian subcontinent and southeast Asia (which, because of continental drift, were in different positions than they are today). Depending on the trajectory of the impacting asteroid or comet, fires may have also struck other parts of those continents and possibly Australia, Antarctica and Europe.

The two worst places to be were the Chicxulub region and, ironically, the place farthest away: India, which 65 million years ago was located on the opposite side of the planet from Chicxulub, making it a focus point for debris. In the hours and days that followed, Earth's rotation carried landmasses to the east, bringing them under the hail of ejected material. Thus, the global wave of wildfire ignition shifted westward, slowly diminishing in intensity.

In most areas, it did not really matter whether vegetation was growing in a dry place or in a humid swamp. Hot temperatures lasted so long that moisture was driven from wet vegetation, like wood in a kiln, and then set ablaze. Did animals panic when the sky began to glow with falling debris? Were they alarmed when the temperatures began to rise? Did they stand completely still, or did they run in some direction— toward water, for example? Mercifully, most animals would have fallen unconscious as the temperatures rose and never felt the fire bursting out in the bushes and trees around them.

In addition to ravaging forests, the fires produced severe air pollution. Soot and impact-generated dust choked the sky over the entire planet, making it impermeable to sunlight. Some calculations suggest that the surface was as dark as a lightless cave, although the precise amount of darkening remains uncertain. In any event, photosynthetic plants died and food chains collapsed, even in areas untouched by wildfires, such as the sea. This phase has been likened to "nuclear winter," a cold spell that some modelers have suggested may follow a nuclear exchange [see "The Climatic Effects of Nuclear War," by Richard P. Turco, Owen B. Toon, Thomas P. Ackerman, James B. Pollack and Carl Sagan; SCIENTIFIC AMERICAN, August 1984]. The dirt took months to wash out, probably falling as blue rain similar to the blue ash-rich rain seen after modern volcanic eruptions.

Cretaceous Park

The climate during the late Cretaceous period, just before the comet or asteroid impact 65 million years ago, was warmer than it is now. No ice covered the polar regions, and some dinosaurs migrated as far north as today's Alaska and as far south as the Seymour Islands of Antarctica. A seaway cut through North America, joining the Gulf of Mexico with the Arctic Ocean. Ecosystems ranged from swamps to deciduous forest. Paleobiologists have mapped out those in North America, where the continental sediments that contain fossils are well preserved. (Little is known about late Cretaceous vegetation in other parts of the world.)

In what is now southern Colorado and northern New Mexico, meandering streams flowed from the nascent Rocky Mountains to a coastal plain in the east. Charles L. Pillmore and his colleagues at the U.S. Geological Survey have mapped several sedimentary settings, including stream channels, overbank deposits, floodplains and swamps. Using fossil leaves in those sediments, Jack Wolfe and Garland Upchurch of the USGS have shown that the vegetation was dominated by near-tropical, broad-leaved evergreen trees that formed an open canopy woodland.

In what is now the Dakotas, Kirk R. Johnson of the Denver Museum of Nature and Science has found fossil leaves that suggest the vegetation was a woodland dominated by angiosperms (flowering plants), mostly small trees (the size of dogwoods) to medium ones (the size of aspen). Wolfe and Upchurch have argued that conditions became wetter farther to the north, supporting a broad-leaved evergreen forest. This forest was denser, and the canopy was probably closed in some areas. Some vines had large leaves with drip tips—long, drawn-out extensions from which water could drain.

Arthur Sweet of the Geological Survey of Canada and his colleagues have shown that, in contrast to the flowering plants that dominated in the U.S., conifers and other cone-bearing plants were the most common in what is now western Canada.

Using modern forest fires as a guide, we have estimated that the conflagrations also released 10,000 billion tons of carbon dioxide, 100 billion tons of carbon monoxide and 100 billion tons of methane—an amount of carbon equivalent to 3,000 years of modern fossil-fuel burning. Therefore, the dark, wintry conditions were followed by an interval of greenhouse warming. The fires also produced debilitating gases such as pyrotoxins, chlorine and bromine, the latter two of which helped to destroy the ozone layer. All these effects dramatically compounded the other environmental consequences of the impact, such as nitric acid rain, sulfuric acid rain, and the vaporization of carbon dioxide stored in rocks at the impact site.

The Day After

The fossil record contains a pattern of ecological disturbance that matches what one would expect from the mother of all wildfires. In the sediments deposited immediately after the impact is a classic biological signature of fire: an anomalously high concentration of fern spores, first seen by Robert H. Tschudy and his colleagues at the U.S. Geological Survey. Ferns (*Cyathidites*) were thus the first plant species to repopulate the denuded landscape—the same pioneering behavior they exhibit when forests are scorched today. The ferns sometimes occurred together with a wind-pollinated flowering plants, *Ulmoideipites*. In some ecosystems without ferns, blooms of algae dominated the postimpact environment.

In sediments deposited in what is now Colorado and Montana, Iain Gilmour and his colleagues at the Open University in England have found chemical and isotopic fingerprints of methane-oxidizing bacteria—a sign that the loss of so much life may have temporarily created anoxic, or oxygen-starved, conditions in small freshwater ecosystems. Although the success of these bacteria is not a signature of fire per se, it does indicate the pervasiveness and abruptness of death, which requires a mechanism such as a global conflagration to explain.

One might ask how anything managed to survive the inferno at all. A crucial factor was the uneven distribution of fire. Simulations indicate, and paleobotanists have confirmed, that northernmost North America and Europe escaped the worst of the devastation. In what is now the Northwest Territories, Arthur Sweet of the Geological Survey of Canada found that the abundance of gymnosperm pollen (from conifers and their relatives) decreased dramatically but did not go to zero. Thus, part of the forest canopy survived the wildfires even in cases where fires consumed the undergrowth, which consisted mostly of angiosperms (flowering plants). In these and other comparatively safe regions, the heat was less intense, so swamps or swamp margins afforded plants and animals some protection.

Based on studies of fossil plants, spores and pollen, Kirk R. Johnson of the Denver Museum of Nature and Science and his colleagues concluded that 51 percent of angiosperm species, 36 percent of gymnosperms, and 25 percent of ferns and fern allies were extinguished in North America. The fossil pollen and leaves suggest that deciduous trees survived better than evergreen trees, perhaps because they could lie dormant.

Trees that were wind-pollinated also seem to have survived better, because they could prosper even if pollinating insects and other animals were exterminated. Indeed, Conrad C. Labandeira of the Smithsonian Institution and his associates have argued that many insects disappeared or went extinct, based on a dramatic drop in the frequency of insect-damaged leaves in the fossil record of North Dakota, which escaped the direct brunt of the impact. Researchers still do not know the detailed effects on other animal species.

Sweet has shown that the initial "survival" ecosystem, dominated by the most robust species, soon gave way to an "opportunistic" ecosystem, composed of a different type of fern (*Laevigatosporites*) and several kinds of flowering plants that were able to take advantage of the ecological clean slate. Together these plants produced an herbaceous ground cover. In the final stage of recovery, the forest canopy returned. Based on observations of modern forests, that regrowth took at least 100 years. Both Sweet and Upchurch have argued that the process was, in fact, far slower—taking up to 10,000 years, judging from the rate at which fossil plants occur in postimpact sediments.

Another measure of the recovery time is the response of the global carbon cycle. The loss of forests, which contain more than 80 percent of aboveground carbon (at least today), and the emission of carbon dioxide from fires and vaporized limestone at the impact site sharply increased the amount of carbon in the atmosphere. In an isotopic analysis of sediments deposited after the impact, Nan C. Arens of the University of California at Berkeley and A. Hope Jahren of Johns Hopkins University concluded that it may have taken 130,000 years for the carbon cycle to return to equilibrium in continental settings. In the marine environment, Steven L. D'Hondt of the University of Rhode Island and other investigators suggest that it took three million years for the flux of organic material to the deep sea to return to normal.

Silent Spring

The world after the Chicxulub impact event looked, smelled and even sounded different. We have all been magically transported to the Amazon and other forests by audio recordings of bird, insect and monkey sounds. If we had a recording from the Cretaceous, we might hear dinosaurs moving through the brush, their calls to one another and the buzz of some insects. Mammals would have been relatively quiet, only rustling among the leaves much as moles do today. But in the months after the impact, the world was far quieter. Wind, flowing water and falling rain dominated the soundscape. Gradually insects, then mammals, could be heard again. Hundreds of years, if not hundreds of thousands of years, were needed for ecosystems to build new, robust architectures.

The firestorm created by the Chicxulub impact and the subsequent pollution were devastating. But it was probably the combination of so many environmental effects that proved to be so deadly. They attacked different ecosystems in different ways on different timescales, ranging from days for reentering ejecta to months for dust in the stratosphere to years for sulfuric acid aerosols.

Life's diversity was its salvation. Although multitudes of species and countless individual organisms were lost, some forms of life survived and proliferated. The impact opened ecological niches for mammalian evolution, which eventually led to the development of our own species. In this sense, the Chicxulub crater is the crucible of human evolution.

The Authors

David A. Kring and Daniel D. Durda met while they were both working at the University of Arizona. Kring was on the team that attributed the Chicxulub crater to an impact and linked it to the Cretaceous/Tertiary mass extinction. Durda was studying the collisional and dynamical evolution of asteroids. Combining their expertise, they worked out the sequence of events that must have unfolded after the impact. Kring is still at Arizona and has studied the environmental effects of nearly two dozen impacts. His favorite haunt is the Barringer Meteorite Crater (a.k.a. Meteor Crater) in Arizona, the world's best preserved impact site. Durda is now at the Southwest Research Institute in Boulder, Colo. He has made astronomical observations from high-performance jet aircraft. An avid pilot, he has logged time in more than a dozen types of aircraft, including the F/A-18 Hornet, and he is also a well-known astronomical artist.

Our planet is not a smooth, round ball. Instead, it is more like a well-used globe with plenty of dents and holes scarring its surface. Some of these geological features are due to natural processes that occur right here on Earth, such as *the previously described volcanic activity. Geologists attribute other marks to asteroid impacts. Asteroids are small, rocky celestial bodies. They are usually found between the planets Mars and Jupiter, but sometimes their orbits cause them to crash into Earth.*

The author of "Repeated Blows" presents her thoughts on dinosaur extinction, but she also discusses the evidence for asteroid impacts. Craters provide the most obvious line of proof. Geologists can tell by examining such depressions on Earth's surface that some rocky object traveling at a high speed must have struck our planet. Additionally, certain rocks, elements, molecules, and even remains of vegetation can hold clues to past impacts. It is sobering to think that, while no major problems associated with asteroids have occurred during our lifetimes, one strong hit could wipe out practically every living thing on Earth. Space agencies, therefore, closely monitor the travel paths of comets, meteors, and other asteroids. —JV

"Repeated Blows"
by Luann Becker
Scientific American, March 2002

Most people are unaware of it, but our planet is under a constant barrage by the cosmos. Our galactic neighborhood is littered with comets, asteroids and other debris left over from the birth of the solar system. Most of the space detritus that strikes the earth is interplanetary dust, but a few of these cosmic projectiles have measured five kilometers (about 3.1 miles) or more across. Based on the number of craters on the moon, astronomers estimate that about 60 such giant space rocks slammed into the earth during the past 600 million years. Even the smallest of those collisions would have left a scar 95 kilometers (about 60 miles) wide and would have released a blast of kinetic energy equivalent to detonating 10 million megatons of TNT.

Such massive impacts are no doubt capable of triggering drastic and abrupt changes to the planet and its inhabitants. Indeed, over the same time period the fossil record reveals five great biological crises in which, on average, more than half of all living species ceased to exist. After a period of heated controversy, scientists began to accept that an asteroid impact precipitated one of these catastrophes: the demise of the dinosaurs 65 million years ago. With that one exception, however, compelling evidence for large impacts coincident with severe mass extinctions remained elusive—until recently.

During the past two years, researchers have discovered new methods for assessing where and when impacts occurred, and the evidence connecting them to other widespread die-offs is getting stronger. New tracers of impacts are cropping up, for instance, in rocks laid down at the end of the Permian period—the time 250 million years ago when a mysterious event known as the Great Dying wiped out 90 percent of the planet's species. Evidence for impacts associated with other extinctions is tenuous but growing stronger as well.

Scientists find such hints of multiple life-altering impacts in a variety of forms. Craters and shattered or shocked rocks—the best evidence of an ancient impact—are turning up at key time intervals that suggest a link with extinction. But more often than not, this kind of physical evidence is buried under thick layers of sediment or is obscured by erosion. Researchers now understand that the biggest blows also leave other direct, as well as indirect, clues hidden in the rock record. The first direct tracers included tiny mineral crystals that had been fractured or melted by the blast. Also found in fallout layers have been elements known to form in space but not on the earth. Indeed, my colleagues and I have discovered extraterrestrial gases trapped inside carbon molecules called fullerenes in several suspected impact-related sediments and craters.

Equally intriguing are the indirect tracers that paleontologists have recognized: rapid die-offs of terrestrial vegetation and abrupt declines in the productivity of marine organisms coincident with at least three of the five great extinctions. Such severe and rapid perturbations in the earth's ecosystem are rare, and some scientists suspect that only a catastrophe as abrupt as an impact could trigger them.

Dinosaur Killer

The first impact tracer linked to a severe mass extinction was an unearthly concentration of iridium, an element that is rare in rocks on our planet's surface but abundant in many meteorites. In 1980 a team from the University of California at Berkeley—led by Nobel Prize–winning physicist Luis Alvarez and his son, geologist Walter Alvarez—reported a surprisingly high concentration of this element within a centimeter-thick layer of clay exposed near Gubbio, Italy. The Berkeley team calculated that the average daily delivery of cosmic dust could not account for the amount of iridium it measured. Based on these findings, the scientists hypothesized that it was fallout from a blast created when an asteroid, some 10 to 14 kilometers (six to nine miles) across, collided with the earth.

Even more fascinating, the clay layer had been dated to 65 million years ago, the end of the Cretaceous period. From this iridium discovery came the landmark hypothesis that a giant impact ended the reign of the dinosaurs—and that such events may well be associated with other severe mass extinctions over the past 600 million years. Twenty years ago this bold and sweeping claim stunned scientists, most of whom had been content to assume that the dinosaur extinction was a gradual process initiated by a contemporaneous increase in global volcanic activity. The announcement led to intense debates and reexaminations of end Cretaceous rocks around the world.

Out of this scrutiny emerged three additional impact tracers: dramatic disfigurations of the earthly rocks and plant life in the form of microspherules, shocked quartz and high concentrations of soot. In 1981 Jan Smit, now at the Free University in Amsterdam, uncovered microscopic droplets of glass, called microspherules, which he argued were products of the rapid cooling of molten rock that splashed into the atmosphere during the impact. Three years later Bruce Bohor and his colleagues at the U.S. Geological Survey were among the first researchers to explain the formation of shocked quartz. Few earthly circumstances have the power to disfigure quartz, which is a highly stable mineral even at high temperatures and pressures deep inside the earth's crust.

At the time microspherules and shocked quartz were introduced as impact tracers, some still attributed them to extreme volcanic activity. Powerful eruptions can indeed fracture quartz grains—but only in one direction, not in the multiple directions displayed in Bohor's samples. The microspherules contained trace elements that were markedly distinct from those formed in volcanic blasts. Scientists subsequently found enhanced iridium levels at more than 100 end Cretaceous sites worldwide and shocked quartz at more than 30 sites.

Least contentious of the four primary impact tracers to come out of the 1980s were soot and ash, which measured tens of thousands of times higher than normal levels, from impact-triggered fires. The most convincing

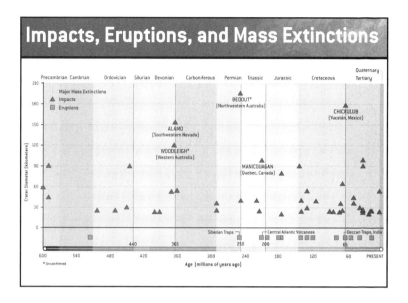

evidence to support the impact scenario, however, was the recognition of the crater itself, known today as Chicxulub, in Yucatán, Mexico. Shortly after the Alvarez announcement in 1980, geophysicists Tony Camargo and Glen Penfield of the Mexican national oil company, PEMEX, reported an immense circular pattern—later estimated to be some 180 kilometers (about 110 miles) across—while surveying for new oil and gas prospects buried in the Gulf of Mexico. Other researchers confirmed the crater's existence in 1991.

Finding a reasonable candidate for an impact crater marked a turning point in the search for the causes of extreme climate perturbations and mass extinctions— away from earthly sources such as volcanism and toward a singular, catastrophic event. Both volcanoes and impacts eject enormous quantities of toxic pollutants such as ash, sulfur and carbon dioxide into the atmosphere, triggering severe climate change and environmental degradation. The difference is in the timing. The instantaneous release from an impact would potentially kill off species in a few thousand years. Massive volcanism, on the other hand, continues to release its pollutants over millions of years, drawing out its effects on life and its habitats.

While geologists were searching for craters and other impact tracers, paleontologists were adding their own momentum to the impact scenario. Fossil experts had long been inclined to agree with the volcanism theory because the disappearance of species in the fossil record appeared to be gradual. A convincing counterargument came from paleontologists Philip Signor of the University of California at Davis and Jere Lipps, now at Berkeley. In 1982 they recognized that the typical approach for defining the last occurrence of a given species did not take into account the incompleteness of the fossil record or the biases introduced in the way the fossils were collected.

Many researchers subsequently conducted high-resolution studies of multiple species. These statistically more reliable assessments indicate that the actual extinction time periods at the end of the Cretaceous—and at the end of the Permian—were abrupt (thousands of years) rather than gradual (millions of years). Although volcanically induced climate change no doubt contributed to the demise of some species, life was well on its way to recovery before the volcanism ceased—making the case for an impact trigger more compelling.

Extraterrestrial Hitchhikers

The recognition of a shorter time frame for the Great Dying prompted several scientists to search for associated impact tracers and craters. By the early 1990s scientific papers were citing evidence of iridium and shocked quartz from end Permian rocks; however, the reported concentrations were 10- to 100-fold lower than those in the end Cretaceous clay. This finding prompted some paleontologists to claim that the impact that marked the end of the age of dinosaurs was as singular and unique as the animals themselves.

Other scientists reasoned that perhaps an impact had occurred but the rocks simply did not preserve the same clues that were so obvious in end Cretaceous samples. At the end of the Permian period the earth's landmasses were configured into one supercontinent, Pangea, and a superocean, Panthalassa. An asteroid or comet that hit the deep ocean would not generate shocked quartz, because quartz is rare in ocean crust. Nor would it necessarily lead to the spread of iridium worldwide, because not as much debris would be ejected into the atmosphere. Supporting an ocean-impact hypothesis for more ancient extinctions such as the Great Dying, it turned out, would require new tracers.

One of the next impact tracers to hit the scene— and one that would eventually turn up in meteorites and at least two impact craters—evolved out of the accidental discovery of a new form of carbon. In the second year of my doctoral studies at the Scripps Institution of Oceanography in La Jolla, Calif., my adviser, geochemist Jeffrey Bada, showed me an article that had appeared in a recent issue of SCIENTIFIC AMERICAN [see "Fullerenes," by Robert F. Curl and Richard E. Smalley; October 1991]. It outlined the discovery of a new form of carbon, closed-cage structures called fullerenes (also referred to as buckminster fullerenes or "buckyballs," after the inventor of the geodesic domes that they resemble). A group of astrochemists and physical chemists had inadvertently created fullerenes in 1985 during laboratory experiments designed to mimic the formation of carbon clusters, or stardust, in some stars. Additional experiments revealed that fullerenes, unlike the other solid forms of carbon, diamond and graphite, were soluble in some organic solvents, a property that would prove their existence and lead to a Nobel Prize in Chemistry for Curl, Smalley and Harold W. Kroto in 1996.

Knowing that stardust, like iridium, is delivered to our planet in the form of cosmic dust, asteroids and comets, we decided to search for these exotic carbon molecules in earthly sediments. We chose a known impact site—the 1.85-billion-year-old Sudbury crater in Ontario, Canada—because of its unique lining of carbon-rich breccia, a mixture of shattered target rocks and other fallout from the blast. (Not unlike the Chicxulub controversy, it took the discovery of shocked quartz and shattercones, features described as shock waves captured in the rock, to convince most scientists that the crater was an impact scar rather than volcanic in origin.)

Because fullerene is a pure-carbon molecule, the Sudbury breccia offered a prime location for collecting promising samples, which we did in 1993. By exploiting the unique solubility properties of fullerene, I was able to isolate the most stable molecules—those built from 60 or 70 carbon atoms each—in the laboratory. The next critical questions were: Did the fullerenes hitch a ride to the earth on the impactor, surviving the catastrophic blast? Or were they somehow generated in the intense heat and pressures of the event?

Meanwhile organic chemist Martin Saunders and his colleagues at Yale University and geochemist Robert Poreda of the University of Rochester were discovering a way to resolve this question. In 1993 Saunders and Poreda demonstrated that fullerenes have the unusual ability to capture noble gases—such as helium, neon and argon—within their caged structures. As soon as Bada and I became aware of this discovery, in 1994, we asked Poreda to examine our Sudbury fullerenes. We knew that the isotopic compositions of noble gases observed in space (like those measured in meteorites and cosmic dust) were clearly distinct from those found on the earth. That meant we had a simple way to test where our exotic carbon originated: measure the isotopic signatures of the gases within them.

What we found astounds us to this day. The Sudbury fullerenes contained helium with compositions similar to some meteorites and cosmic dust. We reasoned that the molecules must have survived the catastrophic impact, but how? Geologists agree that the Sudbury impactor was at least eight kilometers (about five miles) across. Computer simulations predicted that all organic compounds in an asteroid or comet of this size would be vaporized on impact. Perhaps even more troubling was the initial lack of compelling evidence for fullerenes in meteorites.

We, too, were surprised that the fullerenes survived. But as for their apparent absence in meteorites, we suspected that previous workers had not looked for all the known types. In the original experiment designed to simulate stardust, a family of large fullerenes formed in addition to the 60- and 70-atom molecules. Indeed, on a whim, I attempted to isolate larger fullerenes in some carbon-rich meteorites, and a whole series of cages with up to 400 carbon atoms were present. Like their smaller counterparts from the Sudbury crater, these larger structures contained extraterrestrial helium, neon and argon.

With the discovery of the giant fullerenes in meteorites, Poreda and I decided to test our new method on sediments associated with mass extinctions. We first revisited fullerene samples that other researchers had discovered at end Cretaceous sites. One group, led by Dieter Heymann of Rice University, had proposed that the exotic carbon was part of the soot that accumulated in the wake of the massive, impact-ignited fires. The heat of such a fire may have been intense enough to transform plant carbon into fullerenes, but it could not account for the extraterrestrial helium that we found inside them.

Inspired by this success, we wondered whether fullerenes would be a reliable tracer of large impacts elsewhere in the fossil record. Sediments associated with the Great Dying became our next focus. In February 2001 we reported extraterrestrial helium and argon in fullerenes from end Permian locations in China and Japan. In the past several months we have also begun to look at end Permian sites in Antarctica. Preliminary investigations of samples from Graphite Peak indicate that fullerenes are present and contain extraterrestrial helium and argon. These end Permian fullerenes are also associated with shocked quartz, another direct indicator of impact.

As exciting as these new impact tracers linked to the Great Dying have been, it would be misleading to suggest that fullerenes are the smoking gun for a giant impact. Many scientists still argue that volcanism is the more likely cause. Some have suggested that cosmic dust is a better indicator of an impact event than fullerenes are. Others are asking why evidence such as shocked quartz and iridium are so rare in rocks associated with the Great Dying and will remain skeptical if an impact crater cannot be found.

Forging Ahead

Undaunted by skepticism, a handful of scientists continues to look for potential impact craters and tracers. Recently geologist John Gorter of Agip Petroleum in Perth, Australia, described a potential, enormous end Permian impact crater buried under a thick pile of sediments offshore of northwestern Australia. Gorter interpreted a seismic line over the region that suggests a circular structure, called the Bedout, some 200 kilometers (about 125 miles) across. If a future discovery of shocked quartz or other impact tracers proves this structure to be ground zero for a life-altering impact, its location could explain why extraterrestrial fullerenes are found in China, Japan and Antarctica—regions close to the proposed impact—but not in more distant sites, such as Hungary and Israel.

Also encouraging are the recent discoveries of other tracers proposed as direct products of an impact. In September 2001 geochemist Kunio Kaiho of Tohoku University in Japan and his colleagues reported the presence of impact-metamorphosed iron-silica-nickel grains in the same end Permian rocks in Meishan, China, where evidence for abrupt extinctions and extraterrestrial fullerenes has cropped up. Such grains have been reported in several end Cretaceous impact sites around the world as well.

In the absence of craters or other direct evidence, it still may be possible to determine the occurrence of an impact by noting symptoms of rapid environmental or biological changes. In 2000, in fact, Peter Ward of the University of Washington and his colleagues reported evidence of abrupt die-offs of rooted plants in end Permian rocks of the Karoo Basin in South Africa.

Several groups have also described a sharp drop in productivity in marine species associated with the Great Dying—and with the third of the five big mass extinctions, in some 200-million-year-old end Triassic rocks. These productivity crashes, marked by a shift in the values of carbon isotopes, correlate to a similar record at the end of the Cretaceous, a time when few scientists doubt a violent impact occurred.

Only more careful investigation will determine if new impact tracers—both direct products of a collision and indirect evidence for abrupt ecological change—will prove themselves reliable in the long run. So far researchers have demonstrated that several lines of evidence for impacts are present in rocks that record three of our planet's five most devastating biological crises. For the two other largest extinctions—one about 440 million years ago and the other about 365 million years ago—iridium, shocked quartz, microspherules, potential craters and productivity collapse have been reported, but the causal link between impact and extinction is still tenuous at best. It is important to note, however, that the impact tracers that typify the end of the Cretaceous will not be as robust in rocks linked to older mass extinctions.

The idea that giant collisions may have occurred multiple times is intriguing in its own right. But perhaps even more compelling is the growing indication that these destructive events may be necessary to promote evolutionary change. Most paleontologists believe that the Great Dying, for instance, enabled dinosaurs to thrive by opening niches previously occupied by other animals. Likewise, the demise of the dinosaurs allowed mammals to flourish. Whatever stimulated these mass extinctions, then, also made possible our own existence. As researchers continue to detect impact tracers around the world, it's looking more like impacts are the culprits of the greatest unresolved murder mysteries in the history of life on earth.

The Author

Luann Becker has studied impact tracers since she began her career as a geochemist at the Scripps Institution of Oceanography in La Jolla, Calif., in 1990. In 1998, Becker participated in a meteorite-collecting expedition in Antarctica, and in July 2001 was awarded the National Science Foundation Antarctic Service Medal. The following month, she joined the faculty at the University of California, Santa Barbara, where she continues to study fullerenes and exotic gases trapped within them as impact tracers.

In the following article, the authors describe how geologists can utilize data on geological evidence associated with asteroid impacts to re-create past events. They focus on a site called Wabar in the Saudi Arabian desert. What makes this story especially intriguing is that the asteroid event could have taken place as little as just over 100 years ago.

Based on all of the physical evidence, they describe what might have happened at Wabar. In one section, they compare the asteroid hit to the nuclear bomb that exploded in Hiroshima, Japan, during World War II. Incredibly, both the asteroid and the bomb released the same amount of energy, only the asteroid broke into pieces and involved an airburst, as opposed to Hiroshima's direct ground hit. Imagine if such an asteroid did not break up and then hit a highly populated region, instead of a remote desert. The casualties could run into the millions. As a result, researchers continue not only to monitor asteroids but also to explore ways of destroying or diverting them if they threaten to collide with our planet. —JV

"The Day the Sands Caught Fire"
by Jeffrey C. Wynn and Eugene M. Shoemaker
Scientific American, November 1998

Imagine, for a moment, that you are standing in the deep desert, looking northwest in the evening twilight. The landscape is absolutely desolate: vast, shifting dunes of grayish sand stretch uninterrupted in all directions. Not a rock is to be seen, and the nearest other human being is 250 kilometers away. Although the sun has set, the air is still rather warm—50 degrees Celsius—and the remnant of the afternoon sandstorm is still stinging your back. The prevailing wind is blowing from the south, as it always does in the early spring.

Suddenly, your attention is caught by a bright light above the darkening horizon. First a spark, it quickly brightens and splits into at least four individual streaks. Within a few seconds it has become a searing flash. Your clothes burst into flames. The bright objects flit silently over your head, followed a moment later by a deafening crack. The ground heaves, and a blast wave flings you forward half the length of a football field. Behind you, sheets of incandescent fire erupt into the evening sky and white boulders come flying through the air. Some crash into the surrounding sand; others are engulfed by fire.

Glowing fluid has coated the white boulders with a splatter that first looks like white paint but then turns progressively yellow, orange, red and finally black as it solidifies—all within the few seconds it takes the rocks to hit the ground. Some pieces of the white rock are fully coated by this black stuff; they metamorphose into a frothy, glassy material so light that it could float on water, if there were any water around. A fiery mushroom cloud drifts over you now, carried by the southerly breeze, blazing rainbow colors magnificently. As solid rocks become froth and reddish-black molten glass rains down, you too become part of the spectacle— and not in a happy way.

Deep in the legendary Empty Quarter of Saudi Arabia—the Rub' al-Khali—lies a strange area, half a square kilometer (over 100 acres) in size, covered with black glass, white rock and iron shards. It was first described to the world in 1932 by Harry St. John "Abdullah" Philby, a British explorer perhaps better known as the father of the infamous Soviet double-agent Kim Philby. The site he depicted had been known to several generations of roving al-Murra Bedouin as *al-Hadida*, "the iron things."

There is a story in the Qur'an, the holy book of Islam, and in classical Arabic writings about an idolatrous king named Aad who scoffed at a prophet of God. For his impiety, the city of Ubar and all its inhabitants were destroyed by a dark cloud brought on the wings of a great wind. When Philby's travels took him to the forbidding Empty Quarter, his guides told him that they had actually seen the destroyed city and offered to take him there. Philby gladly accepted the offer to visit what he transliterated in his reports as "Wabar," the name that has stuck ever since.

What he found was neither the lost city of Ubar nor the basis for the Qur'anic story. But it was certainly the setting of a cataclysm that came out of the skies: the arrival of a meteorite. Judging from the traces left behind, the crash would have been indistinguishable from a nuclear blast of about 12 kilotons, comparable to the Hiroshima bomb. It was not the worst impact to have scarred our planet over the ages. Yet Wabar holds a special place in meteor research. Nearly all known hits on the earth have taken place on solid rock or on rock covered by a thin veneer of soil or water. The Wabar impactor, in contrast, fell in the middle of the largest contiguous sand sea in the world. A dry, isolated place, it is perhaps the best-preserved and geologically simplest meteorite site in the world. Moreover, it is one of only 17 locations—out of a total of nearly 160 known impact structures—that still contain remains of the incoming body.

In three grueling expeditions to the middle of the desert, we have reconstructed the sequence of events at Wabar. The impact was an episode much repeated throughout the earth's geologic and biological history. And the solar system has not ceased to be a shooting gallery. Although the biggest meteors get most of the attention, at least from Hollywood, the more tangible threat to our cities comes from smaller objects, such as the one that produced Wabar. By studying Wabar and similarly unfortunate places, researchers can estimate how often such projectiles strike the earth. If we are being shot at, there is some consolation in knowing how often we are being shot at.

One has to wonder how Philby's Bedouin guides knew about Wabar, which is found in the midst of a colossal dune field without any landmarks, in a land-scape that changes almost daily. Even the famously tough desert trackers shy away from the dead core of the Empty Quarter. It took Philby almost a month to get there. Several camels died en route, and the rest were pushed to their limits. "They were a sorry sight indeed on arrival at Mecca on the ninetieth day, thin and humpless and mangy," Philby told a meeting of the Royal Geographical Society on his return to London in 1932.

Otherworldly

When he first laid eyes on the site, he had become only the second Westerner (after British explorer Bertram Thomas) to cross the Empty Quarter. He searched for human artifacts, for the remains of broken walls. His guides showed him black pearls littering the ground, which they said were the jewelry of the women of the destroyed city. But Philby was confused and disappointed. He saw only black slag, chunks of white sandstone and two partially buried circular depressions that suggested to him a volcano. One of his guides brought him a piece of iron the size of a rabbit. The work of the Old People? It slowly dawned on Philby that this rusty metal fragment was not from this world. Laboratory examination later showed that it was more than 90 percent iron, 3.5 to 5 percent nickel and four to six parts per million iridium—a so-called sidereal element only rarely found on the earth but common in meteorites.

The actual site of the city of Ubar, in southern Oman about 400 kilometers (250 miles) south of Philby's Wabar, was uncovered in 1992 with the help of satellite images [see "Space Age Archaeology," by Farouk El-Baz; SCIENTIFIC AMERICAN, August 1997]. Wabar, meanwhile, remained largely unexplored until our expeditions in May 1994, December 1994 and

March 1995. The site had been visited at least twice since 1932 but never carefully surveyed.

It was not until our first trip that we realized why. One of us (Wynn) had tagged along on an excursion organized by Zahid Tractor Corporation, a Saudi dealer of the Hummer vehicle, the civilian version of the military Humvee. To promote sales of the vehicle, a group of Zahid managers, including Bill Chasteen and Wafa Zawawi, vowed to cross the Empty Quarter and invited the U.S. Geological Survey mission in Jeddah to send a scientist along. This was no weekend drive through the countryside; it was a major effort requiring special equipment and two months of planning. No one had ever crossed the Empty Quarter in the summer. If something went wrong, if a vehicle broke down, the caravan would be on its own: the long distance, high temperatures and irregular dunes preclude the use of rescue helicopters or fixed-wing aircraft.

An ordinary four-wheel-drive vehicle would take three to five days to navigate the 750 kilometers from Riyadh to Wabar. It would bog down in the sand every 10 minutes or so, requiring the use of sand ladders and winches. A Hummer has the advantage of being able to change its tire pressure while running. Even so, the expedition drivers needed several days to learn how to get over dunes. With experience, the journey to Wabar takes a long 17 hours. The last several hours are spent crossing the dunes and must be driven in the dark, so that bumper-mounted halogen beams can scan for the unpredictable 15-meter sand cliffs.

Our first expedition stayed at the site for a scant four hours before moving on. By that time, only four of the six vehicles still had working air conditioners. Outside, the temperature was 61 degrees C (142 degrees Fahrenheit)—in the shade under a tarp—and the humidity was 2 percent, a tenth of what the rest of the world calls dry. Wynn went out to do a geomagnetic survey, and by the time he returned he was staggering and speaking an incoherent mixture of Arabic and English. Only some time later, after water was poured on his head and cool air was blasted in his face, did his mind clear.

Zahid financed the second and third expeditions as well. On our weeklong third expedition, furious sandstorms destroyed our camp twice, and the temperature never dropped below 40 degrees C, even at night. We each kept a two-liter thermos by our beds; the burning in our throats awoke us every hour or so.

Shocking Rock

The Wabar site is about 500 by 1,000 meters in size. There are at least three craters, two (116 and 64 meters wide) recorded by Philby and the other (11 meters wide) by Wynn on our second expedition. All are nearly completely filled with sand. The rims we now see are composed of heaped-up sand, anchored in place both by "impactite" rock—a bleached, coarse sandstone— and by large quantities of black-glass slag and pellets. These sandy crater rims are easily damaged by tire tracks. There are also occasional iron-nickel fragments.

Identifying Impact Craters

How would you recognize an impact crater if you fell into one? It isn't easy. Although the moon is covered with craters, it has no water, no weather, no continental drift—so the craters just stay where they formed, barely changed over the aeons. On the earth, however, all these factors have erased what would otherwise have been an equally pockmarked surface. To confuse matters further, more familiar processes—such as volcanism and erosion—also leave circular holes. Not until early this century did geologists first confirm that some craters are caused by meteorites. Even today there are only about 160 known impact structures.

Only about 2 percent of the asteroids floating around in the inner solar system are made of iron and nickel, whose fragments are fairly easy to recognize as foreign. But other types of meteorites blend in with the rest of the stones on the ground. The easiest place to pick them out is in Antarctica, because few other rocks find their way to the middle of an ice field. Elsewhere, recognizing a meteorite crater requires careful mapping and laboratory work. Geologists look for several distinctive features, which result from the enormous velocities and pressures involved in an impact. Even a volcanic eruption does not subject rocks to quite the same conditions.

Geologists can deduce that a crater was produced by meteorite impact—rather than by other processes such as erosion or volcanism—by looking for signs that shock waves have passed through rocks. The impactite rocks at the Wabar site pass the test. They are coarsely laminated, like other sandstones, but these laminations consist of welded sand interspersed with ribbonlike voids. Sometimes the layers all bend and twist in unison, unlike those in any other sandstone we have ever seen. The laminations are probably perpendicular to the path taken by a shock wave. Moreover, the impactite contains coesite, a form of shocked quartz found only at nuclear blast zones and meteorite sites. X-ray diffraction experiments show that coesite has an unusual crystal structure, symptomatic of having experienced enormous pressures.

The impactite is concentrated on the southeastern rims and is almost entirely absent on the north and west sides of the craters. This asymmetry suggests that the impact was oblique, with the incoming objects arriving from the northwest at an angle between 22 and 45 degrees from the horizontal.

The two other types of rock found at Wabar are also telltale signs of an impact. Iron-nickel fragments are practically unknown elsewhere in the desert, so they are probably remnants of the meteorite itself. The fragments come in two forms. When found beneath the sand, they are rusty, cracked balls up to 10 centimeters in diameter that crumble in the hand. Daniel M. Barringer, an

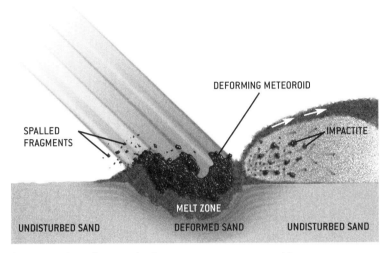

Cross section of meteorite impact, as reconstructed by computer simulations, shows how the Wabar craters were created within a matter of seconds. The meteorite flattened as it hit the ground; a shock wave traveled backward through the body, causing part of it to spall off with little damage; the rest of the meteorite melted and amalgamated with sand directly underneath; surrounding sand was compressed into impactite. The whole mess was then thrust into the air. Deeper layers of sand were relatively unaffected.

American mining engineer who drilled for iron at Meteor Crater in Arizona early this century, called such fragments, which occur at several iron-meteor sites, "shale balls."

When the iron fragments are found at the surface, they are generally smooth, covered with a thin patina of black desert varnish. The largest piece of iron and nickel is the so-called Camel's Hump, recovered in a 1965 expedition and now displayed at King Saud University in Riyadh. This flattened, cone-shaped chunk, weighing 2,200 kilograms (2.43 tons), is probably a fragment that broke off the main meteoroid before impact. Because the surface area of an object is proportional to its radius squared, whereas mass is proportional to the radius cubed, a smaller object undergoes proportionately more air drag. Therefore, a splinter from the projectile slows down more than the main body; when it lands, it may bounce rather than blast out a crater.

The other distinctive type of rock at Wabar is the strange black glass. Glassy rock is often found at impact sites, where it is thought to form from molten blobs of material splattered out from the crater. Near the rims of the Wabar craters, the black glass looks superficially like Hawaiian pahoehoe, a ropy, wrinkled rock that develops as thickly flowing lava cools. Farther away, the glass pellets become smaller and more drop-like. At a distance of 850 meters northwest of the nearest crater, the pellets are only a few millimeters across; if there are any pellets beyond this distance, sand dunes have covered them. When chemically analyzed, the glass is uniform in content: about 90 percent local sand and 10 percent iron and nickel. The iron and nickel appear as microscopic globules in a matrix of melted sand. Some of the glass is remarkably fine. We have found filigree glass-splatter so fragile that it does not survive transport from the site, no matter how well packaged.

The glass distribution indicates that the wind was blowing from the southeast at the time of impact. The wind direction in the northern Empty Quarter is seasonal. It blows from the north for 10 months of the year, sculpting the huge, horned barchan sand dunes. But during the early spring, the wind switches direction to come from the southeast. Spring is the desert sandstorm season that worried military planners during the Gulf War; it coincides with the monsoon season in the Arabian Sea. All year long, the air is dead still when the sun rises, but it picks up in the early afternoon. By sunset it is blowing so hard that sand stings your face as you walk about; on our expeditions, we needed swim goggles to see well enough to set up our tents. Around midnight the wind drops off again.

Curtains

Black material and white—the Wabar site offers little else. This dichotomy suggests that a very uniform process created the rocks. The entire impact apparently took place in sand; there is no evidence that it penetrated down to bedrock. In fact, our reconnaissance found no evidence of outcropping rock (bedrock that reaches the surface) anywhere within 30 kilometers.

From the evidence we accumulated during our expeditions, as well as from the modeling of impacts by H. Jay Melosh and Elisabetta Pierazzo of the University of Arizona, we have pieced together the following sequence of events at Wabar.

The incoming object came from the northwest at a fairly shallow angle. It may have arrived in the late afternoon or early evening, probably during the early spring. Like most other meteoroids, it entered the atmosphere at 11 to 17 kilometers per second (24,600 to 38,000 miles per hour). Because of the oblique angle of its path, the body took longer to pass through the atmosphere than if it had come straight down. Consequently, air resistance had a greater effect on it. This drag force built up as the projectile descended into ever denser air. For most meteoroids, the drag overwhelms the rock strength by eight to 12 kilometers' altitude, and the object explodes in midair. The Wabar impactor, made of iron, held together longer. Nevertheless, it eventually broke up into at least four pieces and slowed to half its initial speed. Calculations suggest a touchdown velocity of between five and seven kilometers per second, about 20 times faster than a speeding .45-caliber pistol bullet.

The general relation among meteorite size, crater size and impact velocity is known from theoretical models, ballistics experiments and observations of nuclear blasts. As a rule of thumb, craters in rock are 20 times as large as the objects that caused them; in sand, which absorbs the impact energy more efficiently, the factor is closer to 12. Therefore, the largest object that hit Wabar was between 8.0 and 9.5 meters in diameter, assuming that the impact velocity was seven or five kilometers per second, respectively. The aggregate mass of the original meteoroid was at least 3,500 tons. Its original kinetic energy amounted to about 100 kilotons of exploding TNT. After the air braking, the largest piece hit with an energy of between nine and 13 kilotons. Although the Hiroshima bomb released a comparable amount of energy, it destroyed a larger area, mainly because it was an airburst rather than an explosion at ground level.

At the point of impact, a conelike curtain of hot fluid—a mixture of the incoming projectile and local sand—erupted into the air. This fluid became the black glass. The incandescent curtain of molten rock expanded rapidly as more and more of the meteorite made contact with the ground. The projectile itself was compressed and flattened during these first few milliseconds. A shock wave swept back through the body; when it reached the rear, small pieces were kicked off—spalled off, in geologic parlance—at gentle speeds. Some of these pieces were engulfed by the curtain, but most escaped and plopped down in the surrounding sand as far as 200 meters away. They are pristine remains of the original meteorite. (Spalling can also throw off pieces of the planet's surface without subjecting them to intense heat and pressure. The famous Martian meteorites, for example, preserved their delicate microstructures despite being blasted into space.)

A shock wave also moved downward, heating and mixing nearby sand. The ratio of iron to sand in the glass pellets suggests that the volume of sand melted was 10 times the size of the meteorite—implying a hemisphere of sand about 27 meters in diameter. Outside this volume, the shock wave, weakened by its progress, did not melt the sand but instead compacted it into "insta-rock": impactite.

The shock wave then caused an eruption of the surface. Some of the impactite was thrown up into the molten glass and was shocked again. In rock samples this mixture appears as thick black paint splattered on the impactite. Other chunks of impactite were completely immersed in glass at temperatures of 10,000 to 20,000 degrees Celsius. When this happened, the impactite underwent a second transition into bubbly glass.

The largest crater formed in a little over two seconds, the smallest one in only four fifths of a second. At first the craters had a larger, transient shape, but within a few minutes material fell back out of the sky, slumped down the sides of the craters and reduced their volume. The largest transient crater was probably 120 meters in diameter. All the sand that had been there was swept up in a mushroom cloud that rose thousands of meters, perhaps reaching the stratosphere. The evening breeze did not have to be very strong to distribute molten glass 850 meters away.

Fading Away

And when did all this take place? That has long been one of the greatest questions about Wabar. The first date assigned to the event, based on fission-track analysis in the early 1970s of glass samples that found their way to the British Museum and the Smithsonian Institution, placed it about 6,400 years ago. Field evidence, however, hints at a more recent event. The largest crater was 12 meters deep in 1932, eight meters deep in 1961 and nearly filled with sand by 1982. The southeastern rim was only about three meters high during our visits in 1994 and 1995. Dune experts believe it would be impossible to empty a crater once filled.

The Wabar site might have already disappeared if impactite and glass had not anchored the sand. At least two of the craters are underlaid by impactite rocks, which represent the original bowl surface before infilling by sand. We were able to collect several samples of sand beneath this impactite lining for thermoluminescence dating. The results, prepared by John Prescott and Gillian Robertson of the University of Adelaide, suggest that the event took place less than 450 years ago.

The most tantalizing evidence for a recent date is the Nejd meteorites, which were recovered after a fireball passed over Riyadh in either 1863 or 1891, depending on which report you believe. The fireball was said to be headed in the direction of Wabar, and the Nejd meteorites are identical in composition to samples from Wabar. So it is likely that the Wabar calamity happened only 135 years ago. Perhaps the grandfathers of Philby's guides saw the explosion from a long way off.

The date is of more than passing interest. It gives us an idea of how often such events occur. The rate of meteorite hits is fairly straightforward to understand:

the bigger they come, the less frequently they fall. The most recently published estimates suggest that something the size of the Wabar impactor strikes the earth about once a decade.

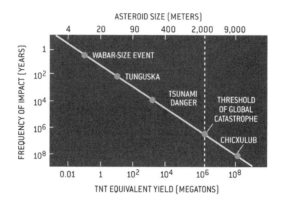

Average frequency of impacts on the earth can be estimated from the amount of scrap material zipping around the solar system and the observed distribution of craters on the moon. A two-kilometer rock, capable of wreaking damage worldwide, falls once every million years on average. (In relating size to explosive energy, this graph assumes a stony asteroid at 20 kilometers per second.)

There are similar iron-meteorite craters in Odessa, Tex.; Henbury, Australia; Sikhote-Alin, Siberia; and elsewhere. But 98 percent of Wabar-size events do not leave a crater, even a temporary one. They are caused by stony meteoroids, which lack the structural integrity of metal and break up in the atmosphere. On the one hand, disintegration has the happy consequence of protecting the ground from direct hits. The earth has relatively few craters less than about five kilometers in diameter; it seems that stony asteroids smaller than 100 to 200 meters are blocked by the atmosphere. On the other hand, this shielding is not as benevolent as it may seem. When objects detonate in the air, they spread their devastation over a wider area. The Tunguska explosion over Siberia in 1908 is thought to have been caused by a stony meteoroid. Although very little of the original object was found on the ground, the airburst leveled 2,200 square kilometers of forest and set much of it on fire. It is only a matter of time before another Hiroshima-size blast from space knocks out a city [see "Collisions with Comets and Asteroids," by Tom Gehrels; SCIENTIFIC AMERICAN, March 1996].

By the standards of known impacts, Wabar and Tunguska are mere dents. Many of the other collision sites around the world, including the Manicouagan ring structure in Quebec, and the Chicxulub site in Mexico's northern Yucatán, are far larger. But such apocalypses happen only every 100 million years on average. The 10-kilometer asteroid that gouged out Chicxulub and snuffed the dinosaurs hit 65 million years ago, and although at least two comparable objects (1627 Ivar and the recently discovered 1998 QS52) are already in earth-crossing orbits, no impact is predicted anytime soon. Wabar-size meteoroids are much more common—and harder for astronomers to spot—than the big monsters. Ironically, until the Wabar expeditions, we knew the least about the most frequent events. The slag and shocked rock in the deserts of Arabia have shown us in remarkable detail what the smaller beasts can do.

The Authors

Jeffrey C. Wynn and Eugene M. Shoemaker worked together at the U.S. Geological Survey (USGS) until Shoemaker's death in a car accident in July 1997. Both geoscientists have something of an Indiana Jones reputation. Wynn, based in Reston, Va., has mapped the seafloor using electrical, gravitational, seismic and remote sensing; has analyzed mineral resources on land; and has studied aquifers and archaeological sites around the world. He served as the USGS resident mission chief in Venezuela from 1987 to 1990 and in Saudi Arabia from 1991 to 1995. His car has broken down in the remote deserts of the southwestern U.S., in the western Sahara and in the deep forest in Amazonas, Venezuela; he has come face-to-snout with rattlesnakes, pit vipers, and camel spiders. Shoemaker, considered the father of astrogeology, was among the first scientists to recognize the geologic importance of impacts. He founded the Flagstaff, Ariz., facility of the USGS, which trained the Apollo astronauts; searched for earth-orbit-crossing asteroids and comets at Palomar Observatory, north of San Diego; and was a part-time professor at the California Institute of Technology. At the time of his death, he was mapping impact structures in the Australian outback with his wife and scientific partner, Carolyn Shoemaker.

Web Sites

Due to the changing nature of Internet links, the Rosen Publishing Group, Inc., has developed an online list of Web sites related to the subject of this book. This site is updated regularly. Please use this link to access the list:

http://www.rosenlinks.com/saca/nadi

For Further Reading

Branley, Franklyn Mansfield. *Dinosaurs, Asteroids, and Superstars*. New York, NY: HarperCollins Children's Books, 1987.

Challoner, Jack. *Eyewitness Hurricane & Tornado*. New York, NY: DK Publishing, 2004.

Drohan, Michele. *Earthquakes*. New York, NY: Rosen Publishing Group, 2003.

Drohan, Michele. *Volcanoes*. New York, NY: Rosen Publishing Group, 2003.

Duden, Jane. *Earthquake! On Shaky Ground*. Logan, IA: Perfection Learning, 1997.

Griffey, Harriet. *DK Readers: Volcanoes and Other Natural Disasters*. New York, NY: DK Publishing, 1998.

Knight, Linsay, and Eldridge Moores. *Volcanoes and Earthquakes*. New York, NY: Time-Life Custom Publishing, 1995.

Lassieur, Allison. *Volcanoes*. Mankato, MN: Capstone Press, 2001.

Meister, Carl, and Cari Meister. *Tornadoes* (Nature's Fury). Edina, MN: ABDO Publishing, 1999.

Nardo, Don. *Comets and Asteroids*. San Diego, CA: Lucent Books, 2003.

Parks, Peggy. *Tsunamis.* Farmington Hills, MI: Thomson Gale, 2005.

Sorenson, Margo, and Kay Ewald. *Hurricane! Nature's Most Destructive Force.* Logan, IA: Perfection Learning, 1997.

Bibliography

Beardsley, Tim. "Dissecting a Hurricane." *Scientific American*, Vol. 282, No. 3, March 2000, pp. 80–85.

Becker, Luann. "Repeated Blows." *Scientific American*, Vol. 286, No. 3, March 2002, pp. 76–83.

Cervelli, Peter. "The Threat of Silent Earthquakes." *Scientific American*, Vol. 290, No. 3, March 2004, pp. 86–91.

Choi, Charles. "Volcanic Sniffing." *Scientific American*, Vol. 291, No. 5, November 2004, pp. 22–24.

Davies-Jones, Robert. "Tornadoes." *Scientific American*, Vol. 273, No. 2, August 1995, pp. 48–57.

Diels, Jean-Claude, Ralph Bernstein, Karl E. Stahlkopf, and Xin Miao Zhao. "Lightning Control with Lasers." *Scientific American*, Vol. 277, No. 2, August 1997, pp. 50–55.

Gantenbein, Douglas. "Burning Questions." *Scientific American*, Vol. 287, No. 5, November 2002, pp. 82–89.

González, Frank I. "Tsunami!" *Scientific American*, Vol. 280, No. 5, May 1999, pp. 56–65.

Holloway, Marguerite. "The Killing Lakes." *Scientific American*, Vol. 282, No. 1, July 2000, pp. 92–99.

Kring, David A., and Daniel D. Durda. "The Day the World Burned." *Scientific American*, Vol. 289, No. 6, December 2003, pp. 98–105.

Mende, Stephen B., Davis D. Sentman, and Eugene M. Westcott. "Lightning Between Earth and Space." *Scientific American*, Vol. 277, No. 2, August 1997, pp. 56–59.

Mukerjee, Madhusree. "The Scarred Earth." *Scientific American*, Vol. 292, No. 3, March 2005, pp. 18–20.

Pfeiffer, Tom. "Mount Etna's Ferocious Future." *Scientific American*, Vol. 288, No. 4, April 2003, pp. 58–65.

Pohl, Otto. "Disease Dustup." *Scientific American*, Vol. 289, No. 1, July 2003, pp. 18–20.

Simpson, Sarah. "Killer Waves on the East Coast?" *Scientific American*, Vol. 283, No. 4, October 2000, pp. 16–17.

Stein, Ross S. "Earthquake Conversations." *Scientific American*, Vol. 288, No. 1, January 2003, pp. 72–79.

Wynn, Jeffrey C., and Eugene M. Shoemaker. "The Day the Sands Caught Fire." *Scientific American*, Vol. 279, No. 5, November 1998, pp. 64–71.

Index

About the Editor

Jennifer Viegas is a news reporter for the Discovery Channel and the Australian Broadcasting Corporation. She also has written for ABC News, *New Scientist*, Knight-Ridder newspapers, the *Christian Science Monitor*, the *Princeton Review*, and several other publications, as well as a number of books for young adults on a variety of science subjects.

Illustration Credits

Cover: Punit Paranjpe/Reuters/Corbis; p. 21 Cornelia Blik; p. 24 (top) Serkan Bozkurt/USGS; p. 24 (bottom) Keith Richards-Dinger/U.S. Navy; p. 25 Shinji Toda/Japan's Active Fault Resource Center; p. 38 David Fierstein; pp. 50–51, 67, 68 (right) Laurie Grace; pp. 56, 73 Jennifer C. Christiansen; p. 68 (left) Aries Galindo; p. 81 (map) Johnny Johnson (image) courtesy of Jeffrey K. Weissel/Lamont-Doherty Earth Observatory; p. 125 Susan Carlson; pp. 155, 157 Bryan Christie; p. 163 Global Atmospherics, Inc./Laurie Grace; p. 167 Alfred T. Kamajian; pp. 192–194 Chris Butler; p. 210 Aaron Firth (based on a graphic by Michael Paine); p. 229 Slim Films; p. 236 David Morrison/NASA Ames Research Center/Laurie Grace.

Series Designer: Tahara Anderson
Series Editor: Wayne Anderson